Foreword

If chess is the sort of game that appeals to you then this book will be the introduction to an amazing world which will live with you all your life. Whether you play the world's worst chess against your family or the best possible chess at international level you will find the game full of endless possibilities.

A few players compete for a living, most just play for fun but everyone plays because they cannot help themselves.

I hope that you will find the step by step method of explanation used in this book easy to understand. I have tried to give all the essential information and to leave out those things which are usually included in books for beginners but which are really only useful to players with experience.

There should be nothing in this book that a beginner cannot completely understand.

A.J.Gillam

Nottingham 1977

Foreword to the Revised Edition

This revised and enlarged edition of *Starting Chess* also contains pages from *Simple Chess Tactics* and *Simple Checkmates* with the intention of taking the reader beyond just the moves of the pieces and rules of the game. The extra material will provide a glimpse into the most fascinating aspect of chess—how the pieces combine together to produce attacks and sacrifices.

A few other changes have been made to make the book both simpler and clearer. This step-by-step guide to playing the game was the first of its type and probably still is the easiest way to learn to play.

A.J.Gillam

Nottingham 2003

R16903

Contents

The Board

Black

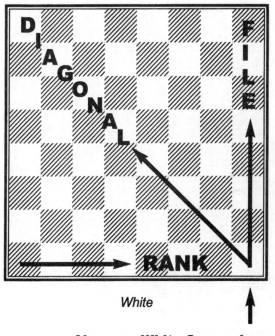

White

Always a White Square here

The Men

This is the starting position of the chess pieces or men. Notice that the two queens stand on the same file and so do the two kings. The easiest way to remember where these pieces start is to remember that each queen starts on her own colour—a black queen on a black square and a white queen on a white square.

You may only have one piece on a square at any time.

White *always* moves first, then Black, then White again and so on. When it's your turn, you *must* move. In all the diagrams in this book, White moves UP the board. This is usual in chess books.

The Bishop

This is how they look in the diagrams in this book.

The Bishop Moves

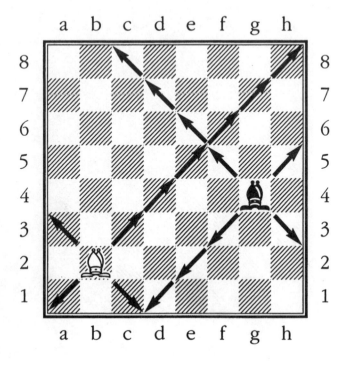

The bishops move on diagonals, backwards or forwards as many squares as they wish but they cannot jump over other chessmen.

The numbers and letters around the diagram are explained on page 31.

The Bishop Moves

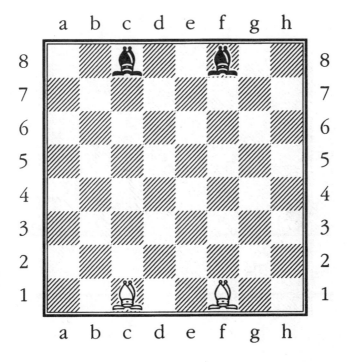

Each bishop moves on squares of one colour only. Both sides have one bishop which moves on white squares and one which moves on black squares. A bishop cannot jump over other chessmen.

In chess, a player can choose whether or not to capture an enemy piece. You do not have to capture and there is no penalty for not capturing.

When a piece is captured it is removed from the board.

The Bishop Takes

Each diagram numbered 1 shows a bishop attacking an enemy piece.

The diagram numbered 2 shows the position after the bishop has made the capture.

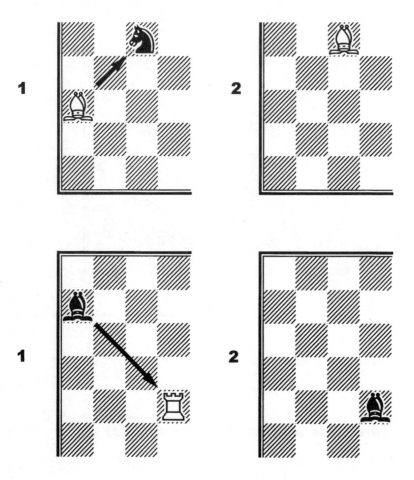

Moving the bishop, capturing the enemy piece and removing it from the board, all counts as one move.

The Rook

This is how they look in the diagrams in this book.

The Rook Moves

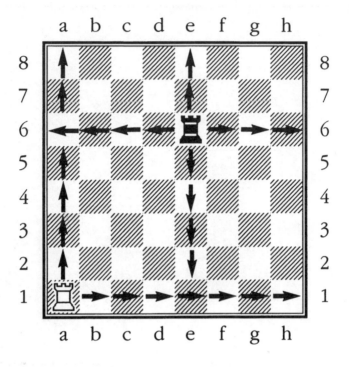

The rook moves in straight lines, up and down or from side to side, as many squares as it wishes but it cannot jump over other chessmen.

The rook can land on both black and white squares.

The Rook Takes

Each diagram numbered 1 shows a rook attacking an enemy piece. The diagram numbered 2 shows the position after the rook has made the capture.

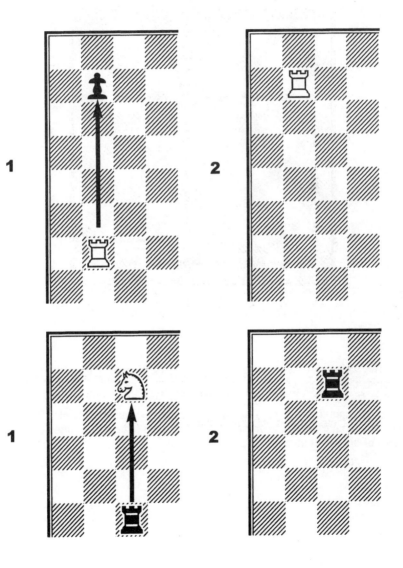

The Rook Takes

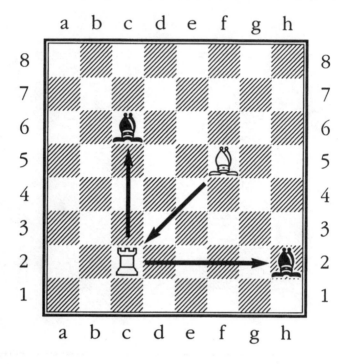

The white rook can take either of the black bishops. The white bishop guards the white rook.

It is important to keep your pieces guarded whenever possible. If your opponent takes one of your pieces then you need to be in a position to take one of his pieces also. So guard your pieces!

The Queen

This is how they look in the diagrams in this book.

The Queen Moves

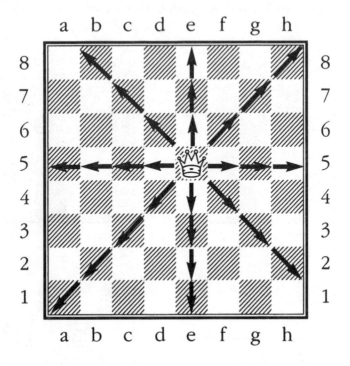

The queen is the strongest chess piece and moves like a bishop and rook together.

The queen can move forwards or backwards and can land on both black and white squares.

The Queen Takes

Each diagram numbered 1 shows a queen attacking an enemy piece. The diagram numbered 2 shows the position after the queen has made the capture.

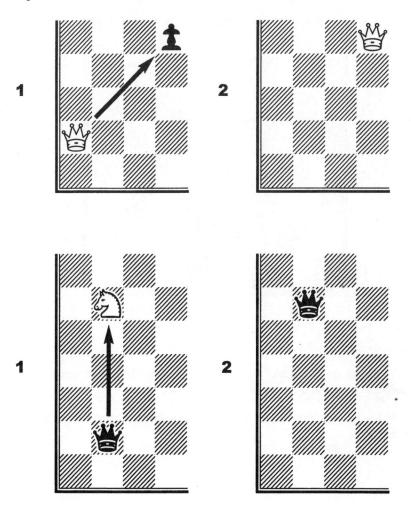

The Queen Takes

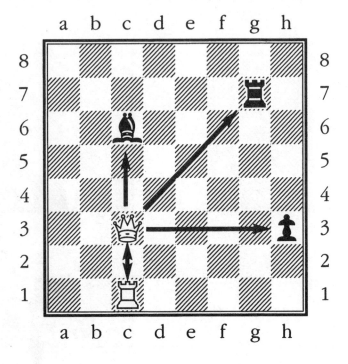

The white queen can take any of the black pieces. The white rook guards the white queen, and the queen guards the rook.

The white rook cannot take the black bishop because it is blocked by its own queen.

The Knight

This is how they look in the diagrams in this book.

The Knight Moves

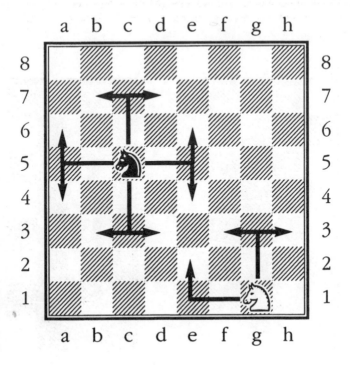

The knight moves two squares forwards and one to the side, or two squares backwards and one to the side, or two squares to the side and one square either up or down.

If a knight starts its move from a white square it will always finish on a black square. If it starts from a black square it will finish on a white one.

Important: The knight jumps over anything in its way without taking it. It is the only piece that jumps over another piece.

The Knight Takes

Each diagram numbered 1 shows a knight attacking an enemy piece. The diagram numbered 2 shows the position after the knight has made the capture.

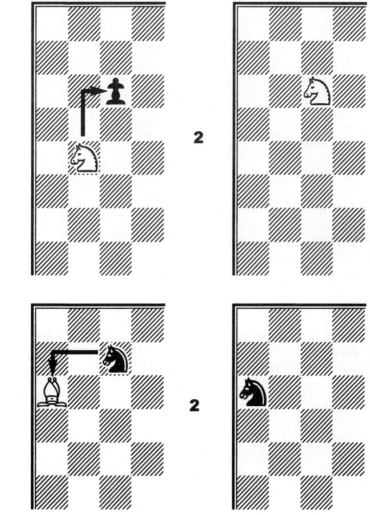

The Knight Takes

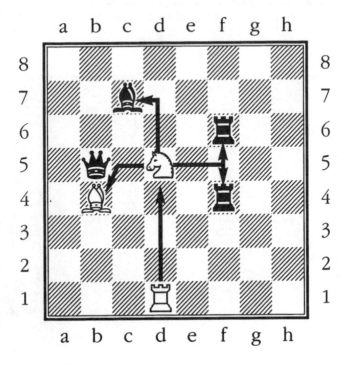

The white knight can take either of the black rooks or the black bishop but not the black queen. The white knight guards the white bishop and the white rook guards the white knight.

The Pawn

This is how they look in the diagrams in this book.

The Pawn Moves

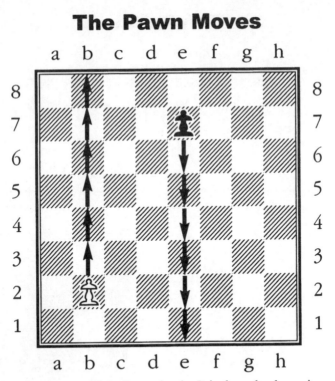

The pawn moves straight forward only. It is the only chess piece which cannot move backwards.

On its first move each pawn may move one or two squares, whichever the player wishes. After its first move a pawn can only move one square at a time.

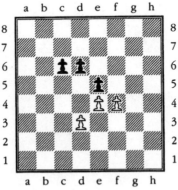

Each pawn in this diagram has made one move only.

26

The Pawn Takes

Although a pawn can only *move* straight ahead, it can only *take* something that is one square away on a diagonal and only in a forward direction.

Each diagram numbered 1 shows a pawn attacking an enemy piece. The diagram numbered 2 shows the position after the pawn has made the capture.

More About The Pawn

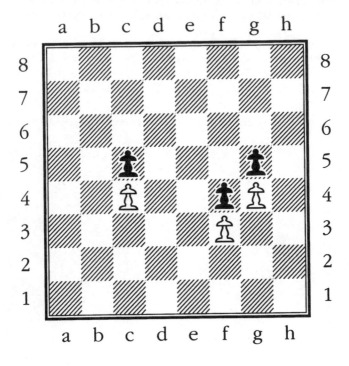

These pawns all block each other. None of them can move or take.

Pawn Promotion

If a pawn reaches the far end of the board, it is 'promoted'. It immediately becomes either a queen, a rook, a bishop or a knight whichever the player wishes.

If, during a game, you play a pawn to the last square on a file (the meaning of the word 'file' is shown on page 7), you remove the pawn and put a promoted piece of your choice on the same square. This is all done as one move.

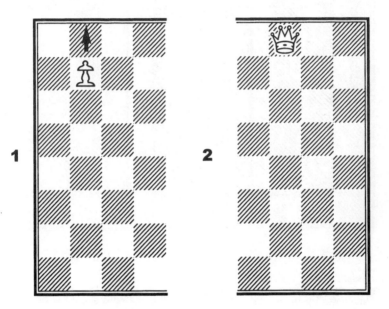

Usually the player chooses to promote the pawn into a queen because that is the strongest piece, That is why we talk about 'queening' a pawn.

By promoting pawns it is possible to have two or more queens or three or more knights, rooks or bishops at the same time.

En Passant

(This is French for 'in passing' and pronounced 'on-pass-on')

This is a special way to capture with a pawn, like this:

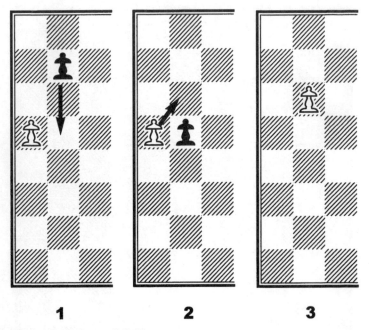

1   **2**   **3**

En passant is *only* possible if:

1 The capturing pawn (the white pawn in the example above) is on the fifth square of a file AND

2 An enemy pawn moves two squares to land on a square by the side of the first pawn. Remember—only if the enemy pawn moves two squares in one move THEN

3 The capturing pawn (the white pawn in our example) may take the enemy pawn, but only on the next move, by pretending it had only moved one square.

Remember—you do not have to take if you do not wish to, but if you wish to take this way, you must do so immediately, because you cannot afterwards. There are more examples later in the book.

Giving Moves a Name

Every square has a name like this:

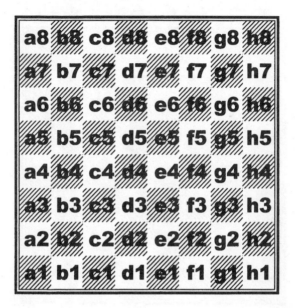

If the white queen moves from d1 to d4 we can write this as Qd1-d4 or just Qd4. We use the letter B for the bishop, R for rook, N for knight and K for king. For the pawns we do not use a letter so if you see the move e4, it means that a pawn has moved to the square e4.

When writing the moves of a game we put in the move numbers as well: 1 e4 e5 2 Nf3 Nc6. This means that on move one White played pawn to e4 and Black replied with pawn to e5. On move two White played knight to f3 and Black played knight to c6.

A capture is written with an 'x' so Rxf3 means that a rook takes whatever is on f3. Check is shown by '+'.

Pawn captures are written by giving the file from which the pawn starts and the square where it finishes e.g. exd4 means a pawn on the e-file takes whatever is on d4.

A good move is shown by a '!' and a bad move by a '?'.

In most modern chess books the moves are printed using a small drawing of the piece (called a figurine) instead of a capital letter. This is the method we will use for the rest of this book.

Practice at Moving and Taking

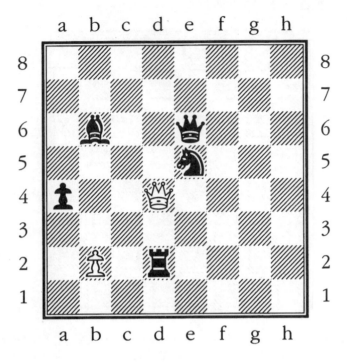

1: Which black pieces can the white queen take?

Bishop, pawn, knight or rook.

2: Which of the black pieces are protected?

Bishop and knight, both by the queen.

3: Where can the white queen move without capturing?

b4, c3, c4, c5, d3, d5, d6, d7, d8, e3, e4, f2, f4, g1, g4, h4.

4: On which of these squares could Black take the white queen?

c4, c5, d3, d5, d6, d7, d8, e3, f2, g1, g4.

In order to avoid capture the white queen can take either the black pawn or the black rook or move to b4, c3, e4, f4 or h4.

Practice at Moving and Taking

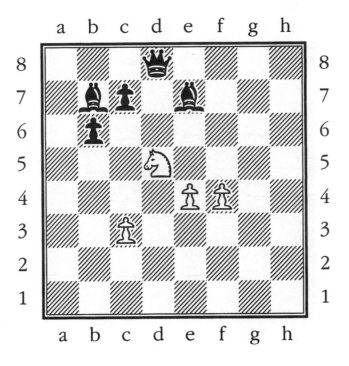

1: What can the knight take?

Either of the black pawns or the bishop on e7.

2: Where else can the knight move?

b4, e3, f6.

3: Where can the knight go without being taken?

e3.

4: Which black piece is not defended?

The bishop on b7, but it isn't attacked either.

Practice at Moving and Taking

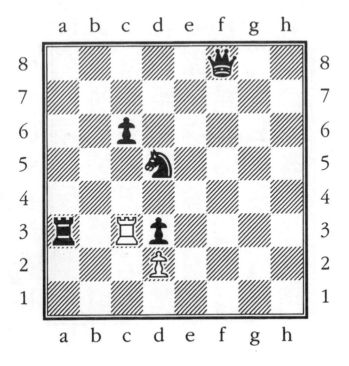

1:   What can the white rook take?

The black rook, the pawn on c6 or the pawn on d3.

2:   Where else can the white rook move?

b3, c1, c2, c4, c5.

3:   Where can the white rook move without being taken?

c1, c4, or take on c6.

4:   Which black pieces are protected?

The rook is protected by the queen, the knight by the pawn on c6 and the pawn on d3 by the rook because if White plays ♖xd3 then Black can reply ♖xd3.

Practice at Moving and Taking

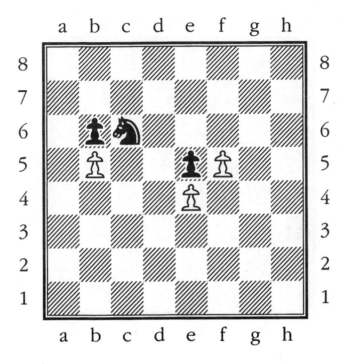

What can the white pawns take?

The pawn on b5 can take the knight on c6. The pawn on e4 cannot move or capture. The pawn on f5 can capture nothing unless Black's last move was e7-e5. If it was, then White can capture 'en passant' which is written f5xe6 or just fxe6.

The black pawns cannot move or capture.

The only other possible pawn move is f6.

Practice at Moving and Taking

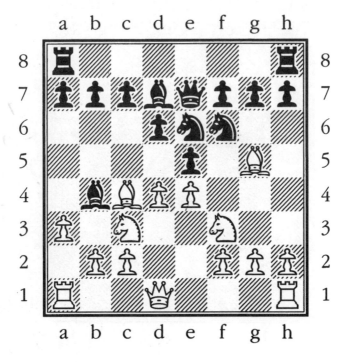

1: Make a list of all possible captures for White.

axb4, dxe5, ♘xe5, ♗xe6, ♗xf6.

2: Make a list of all possible captures for Black.

♗xa3, ♗xc3, ♘xd4, exd4, ♘xe4, ♘xg5.

3: Which white pieces are not protected?

Only the pawns on b2, f2 and g2 and the bishop on c4.

4: Which black pieces are not protected?

The pawn on b7, the bishop on b4 and the queen on e7.

The King

This is how they look in the diagrams in this book.

The king is always the tallest piece in a chess set and usually has a cross at the top.

The King Moves

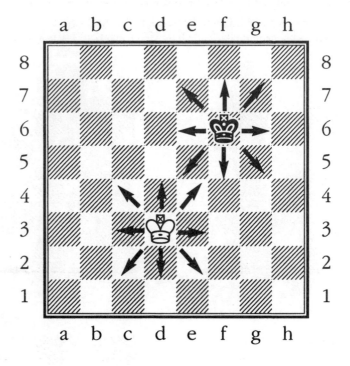

The king moves one square in any direction, except that you cannot move your king into check and there is a special move called castling. Both of these are explained later.

A game of chess is won by the side that captures the enemy king. So if your king is attacked you *must* move it immediately.

The King Takes

Each diagram numbered 1 shows a king attacking an enemy piece.

The diagram numbered 2 shows the position after the king has made the capture. But a king cannot take something if it is guarded (see next page).

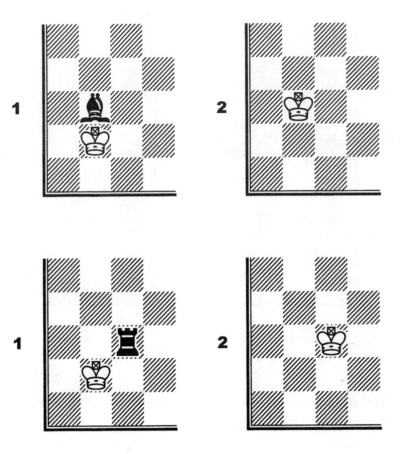

Check

The king is a special piece. When it is attacked, the king is said to be in check. It must get out of check immediately. We write check with a '+'.

If you play a move giving check it is usual to say 'Check'.

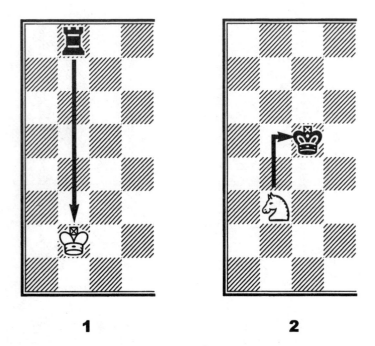

1   **2**

Two examples of check. In both positions the king must immediately move to a square where it is not in check.

In number 1 it can move to a1, a2, a3, c1, c2, or c3, but not b1 or b3 because the king would still be in check. In number 2 it can move to b4, b5, b6, c4, c6, d5, d6, but not d4.

Check

The king is not allowed to move into check or to take anything that is protected.

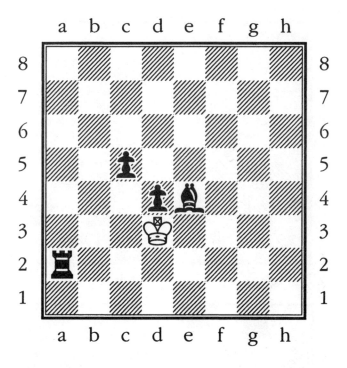

The king is in check and must move. It can take the bishop or move to c4. No other moves are allowed because the king would be moving into check.

Kings that cannot move

Here are some examples of kings that cannot move or capture because they are not allowed to move into check.

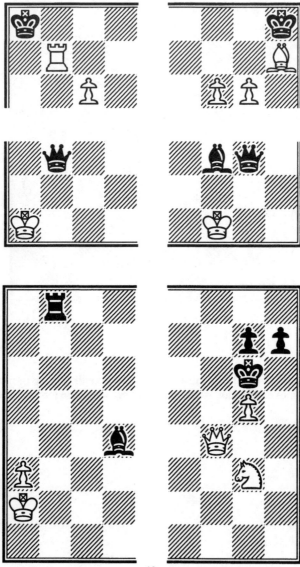

What moves can each King make?

1: The white king can only move to e1 and f1.

2: The black king can only move to d7 because of the white bishop.

All other king moves would be moves into check and so are not allowed.

Where can these Kings move?

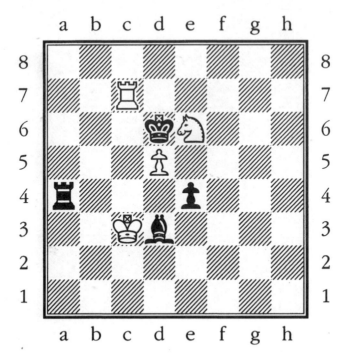

The white king can only move to b2, b3 or d2.

The black king can take the white pawn or move to e5.

No other king move or capture is possible as the kings would be moving into check.

More King Moves

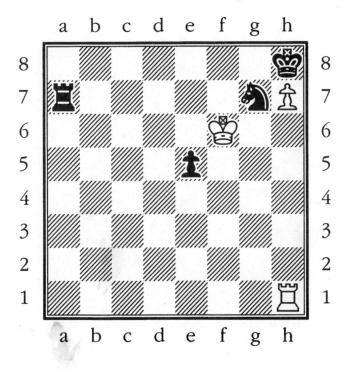

The white king can only take the pawn on e5 or move to g5 or g6.

The black king cannot move or capture.

More King Moves

Neither king can move in this position.

Look carefully and make sure you understand.

Checking the King

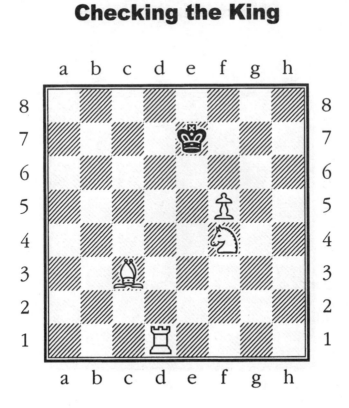

1: How many ways can White give check to the black king?
  ♗b4+, ♗f6+, ♖d7+, ♖e1+, ♘d5+, ♘g6+ and f6+.

2: Which checks can Black answer by taking the checking piece?
  ♗f6+ and ♖d7+.

Checking the King

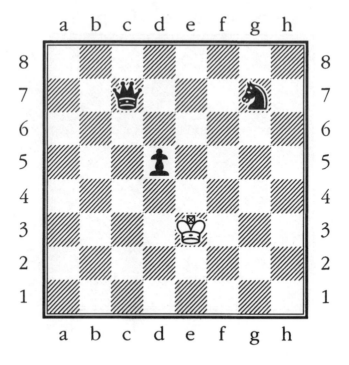

1: How many ways can Black give check to the white king?

♘f5+, d4+ and nine different queen checks on these squares: a7, b6, c1, c3, c5, e5, e7, f4 and g3.

2: Which of these checks could White answer with a capture?

d4+ and ♛f4+.

Discovered Check

This is an example of a special type of check which is very important.

In this position, if Black moves his knight then the white king will be in check from the queen, no matter where the knight goes.

This is called a discovered check.

Discovered Check

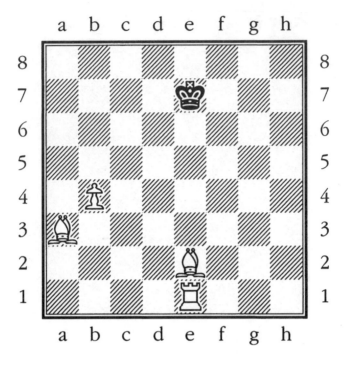

Here White can give a discovered check by moving the pawn or by any move with the bishop on e2.

Double Check

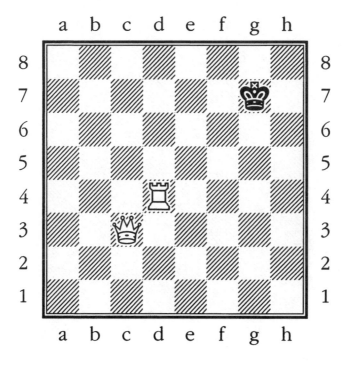

There is a special sort of discovered check when the piece which moves also gives check. So you have two checks at once—a double check.

In the diagram White can double check by ♖d7+ or ♖g4+. All other rook moves give a simple discovered check.

Double Check

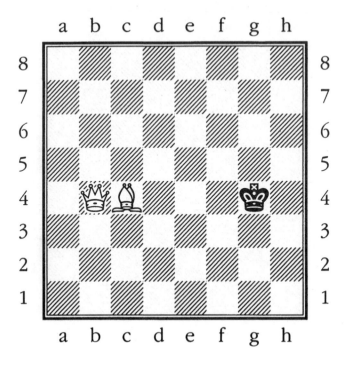

Here ♗e6+ and ♗e2+ are both double checks. Any other bishop move is a discovered check.

Where is the Double Check?

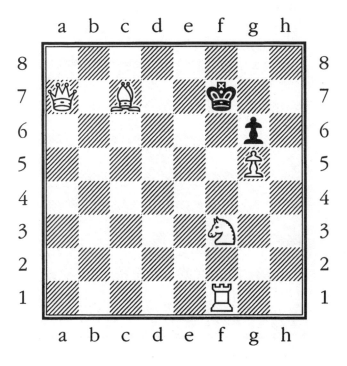

The bishop cannot check the king itself so any bishop move will only be discovered check.

The double check is ♘e5+.

Where is the Discovered Check?

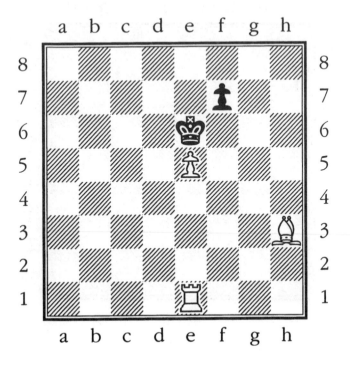

Black is in check from the white bishop. The black king can move out of check to d5 or e7 or Black can play his pawn to f5 to block the check. If Black plays the pawn move then White can reply exf6 (taking 'en passant') which puts Black into double check—from the white rook and white bishop! This is a very unusual type of double check.

Look Again

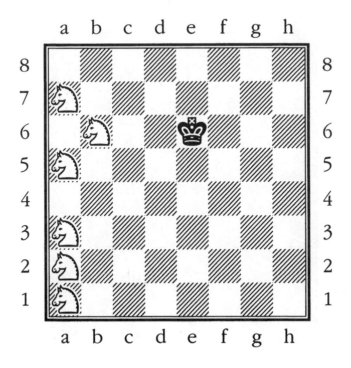

1: How quickly can each knight check the king?

♘a1-b3-c5+ *or* ♘a1-b3-d4+ *or* ♘a1-c2-d4+.

♘a3-c2-d4+ *or* ♘a3-b5-d4+ *or* ♘a3-b5-c7+.

♘a5-b3-c5+ *or* d4+ *or* ♘a5-c6-d8+ *or* d4+ *or* ♘a5-b7-c5+ *or* d8+.

♘b6-d5-f4+ *or* c7+ *or* ♘b6-d7-c5+ *or* f8+ *or* ♘b6-a4-c5+ *or* ♘b6-a8-c7+.

♘a7-b5-d4+ *or* c7+ *or* ♘a7-c6-d4+ *or* d8+.

Look Again

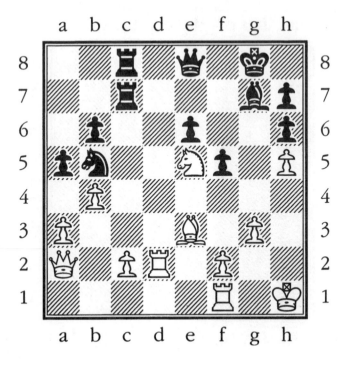

1: What captures can White make?

bxa5, ♛xe6+, ♗xb6, ♗xh6.

2: Which white pieces are not defended?

♛a2, ♘e5, ♖f1, and the pawn on h5.

3: What captures can Black make?

axb4, ♘xa3, ♖xc2, ♗xe5, ♛xh5+.

4: Which black pieces are not defended?

Just the pawn on b6.

Look Again

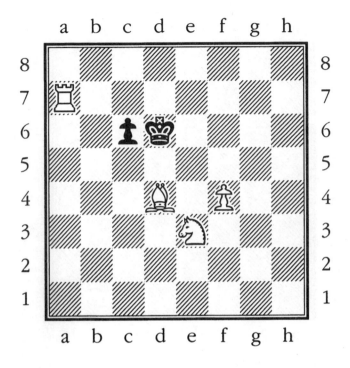

1: How many checks can White play without being taken?

♗e5+, ♘c4+, ♘f5+.

2: If White plays ♗e5+ what can Black play?

Black must get out of check by ♚e6 or ♚c5.

Look Again

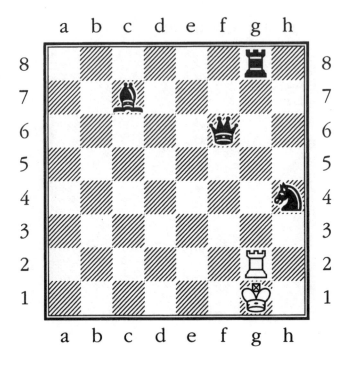

How many ways can Black check without being taken?

♗b6+, ♘f3+, ♖xg2+ *(protected by the knight so White cannot take the rook)*, ♛a1+, ♛b6+, ♛d4+.

If Black plays ♛f2+ then White can capture with his king. He cannot capture with his rook because that would put his king into check from the black rook, see next page.

Pinned Pieces

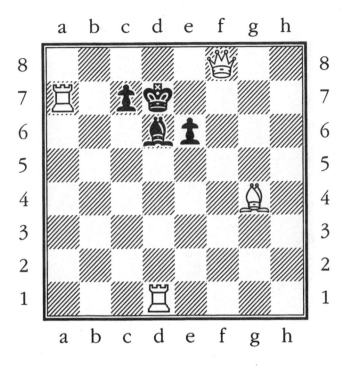

Just as a king may not move into check, no other piece may make a move that would put its own king into check.

In this position the black bishop is 'pinned' because if it moved the white rook on d1 would be checking the king. In the same way the black pawn on c7 is pinned by the other rook and the black pawn on e6 is pnned by the bishop.

Black's only possible move is ♚c6.

Pinned Pieces

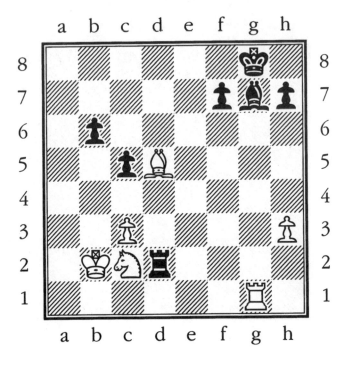

Which pieces are pinned?

White: the knight on c2 and pawn on c3.

Black: the pawn on f7 and bishop on g7.

Pinned Pieces

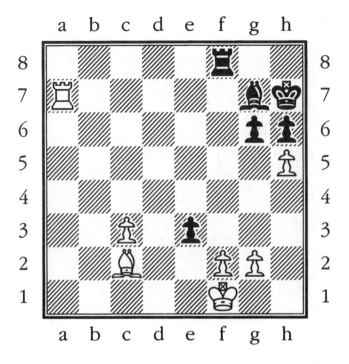

1: What captures can White make?

♖xg7+, ♗xg6+, hxg6+ but not fxe3 because the pawn is pinned.

2: What captures can Black make?

♖xf2+ or exf2 but not ♗xc3 or gxh5 because these men are pinned.

3: Which pieces cannot move or capture in this position?

The black bishop and black pawns on g6 and h6.

The position of the white pawn on f2 is complicated. It cannot take the black pawn on e3 because it is pinned by the black rook, but this pin does not stop the white pawn from moving forward. The pawn can move to f3 or f4 as these moves do not put the white king into check.

Pinned Pieces

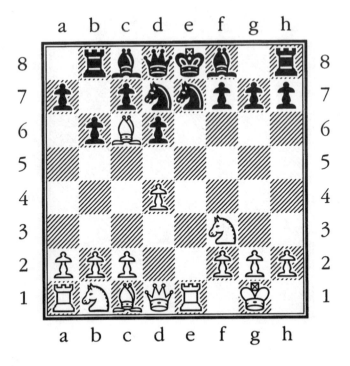

In this position Black's pieces are nearly all pinned or blocked. He can only move his rooks and his bishop on c8 or six of his pawns. Notice that the knight on e7 cannot take the bishop on c6 because of the pin by the rook on e1.

More Checks

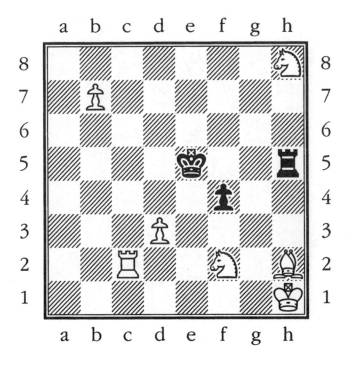

How many ways can you check the black king?

♖c5+, ♖e2+, d4+, ♘g4+, ♘f7+, ♘g6+, b8=♕+ *(the pawn promotes to a queen)* or even b8=♗+ *(the pawn promotes to a bishop).* ♗xf4+ *is not possible because of the pin by the rook on h5.*

More Checks

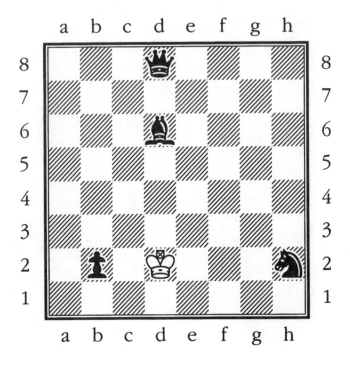

How many ways are there to check the white king?

♘f1+, ♘f3+, ♛a5+, ♛g5+, b1=♘+. Any bishop move gives a discovered check by the queen. ♗b4+ and ♗f4+ are double checks.

Castling—A Special Move

This special move is used by both sides in nearly every game of chess. The idea is to get the king out of the centre of the board where it will be in danger. The different ways of castling are shown below.

(a) Starting position **(b) Finishing position**

1 (a)

1 (b)

2 (a)

2 (b)

3 (a)

3 (b)

4 (a)

4 (b)

Castling

The king moves two squares towards the rook and the rook moves to the square the king has just jumped over. This is all done in *one* move. *Always* move the king first!

You are *not* allowed to castle:

1: If you have previously moved your king even if later you moved it back again.

2: If you are in check. If you can get out of check without moving your king, then you can castle later in the game. You cannot castle to get out of check.

3: If you finish up in check.

4: If your king has to jump over a square where he would be in check.

5: With a rook that has moved, even if you have moved it back again. If one rook has moved then you can still castle with the other rook.

6: If any square between the king and the rook is occupied.

It is important to know these rules exactly so on the next page we give some examples to show when castling is not allowed.

Castling on the King's side (see page 8) is written 0-0 and castling on the Queen's side is written 0-0-0. The move is written the same way whether it is a White or a Black move.

Castling

In all these examples, the king and rook have not moved before, but White cannot castle in any of them.

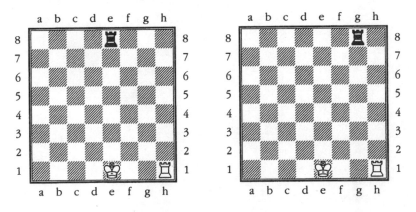

You cannot castle to get out of check or if you will finish in check.

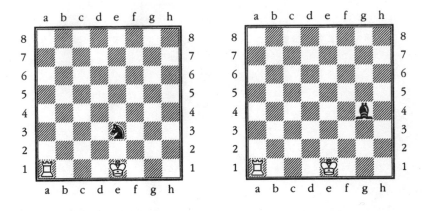

You cannot castle if the square that the king has to jump over is attacked by the enemy. The rook is allowed to jump over an attacked square.

Castling

Black is in check. If he blocks the check by ♝e7 he will be able to castle next move.

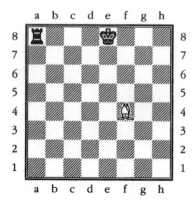

Black is allowed to castle here. The rook may jump over an attacked square (b8 here).

Getting Out of Check

There are three ways to get out of a check.

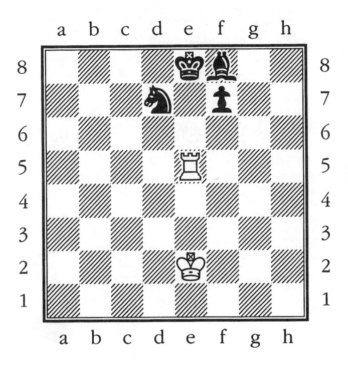

1: Move the king—*♔d8*.

2: Block the check—*♝e7* (but you cannot block a check from a knight).

3: Take the piece giving check—*♞xe5*.

The only way out of a double check is to move the king as you cannot take or block two pieces with one move.

Getting Out of Check

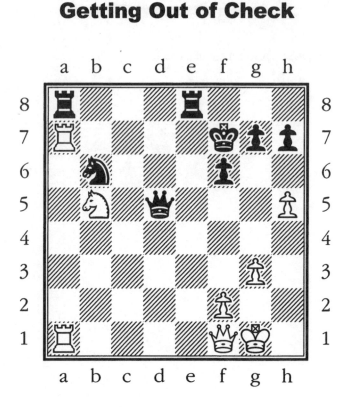

1: How can Black get out of check?

    ♖xa7, ♘d7, ♖e7, ♛b7, ♛d7, ♚g8, ♚f8 or ♚e6.

    One capture, four blocks and three king moves.

2: Which white pieces are not protected?

    Just the pawn on h5.

3: Which black pieces are not protected?

    ♘b6 and the pawn on h7.

Of the three unprotected pieces only the pawn on h5 is attacked.

Getting Out of Check

Black is in check from the knight on e5.

How many ways can Black get out of check?

By taking the knight—♘xe5 or ♗xe5. By moving the king—♚e6, ♚e7, ♚e8, ♚f8 or ♚g8.

You cannot block a check from a knight because the knight can jump over any piece.

Getting Out of Check

The white king is attacked by both the black rook and the black bishop.

How can White get out of this double check?

Only by playing ♔g1. Any other move will still leave him in check from either the rook or the bishop.

Getting Out of Check

Black is in check from the pawn at f6.

How can Black get out of the check?

♘xf6, ♗xf6, ♚g8, ♚h8 or ♚h7.

    If Black just moves the king then White can play fxe7 so it is better for Black to take the pawn with either his bishop or knight. White will not be able to reply exf6+ because his pawn on e5 is pinned.

Getting Out of Check

The black king can get out of check by ♔xe7 or ♔f8, nothing else.

The white king gets out of check by ♕e2 or ♔f1 but not by castling.

How to Win a Game

You win a game of chess by getting the enemy king in *checkmate*. This is a check which he has no way of escaping. This means that no matter what move he plays, you would be able to capture his king next move. His king is lost.

On the next few pages we give some examples of checkmates. Look at them carefully.

Queen Checkmates

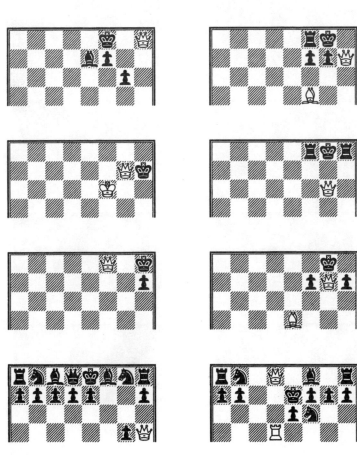

Rook Checkmates

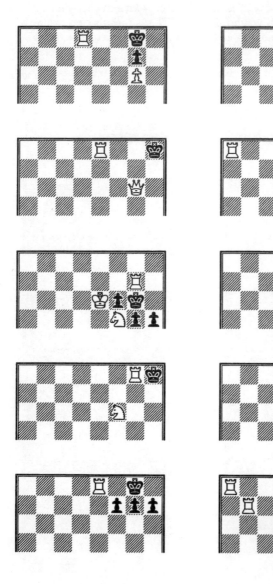

Bishop Checkmates

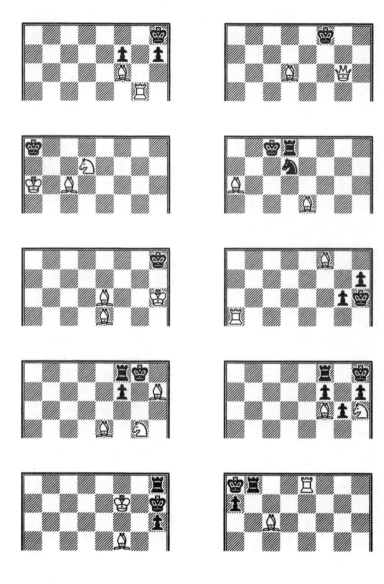

Knight Checkmates

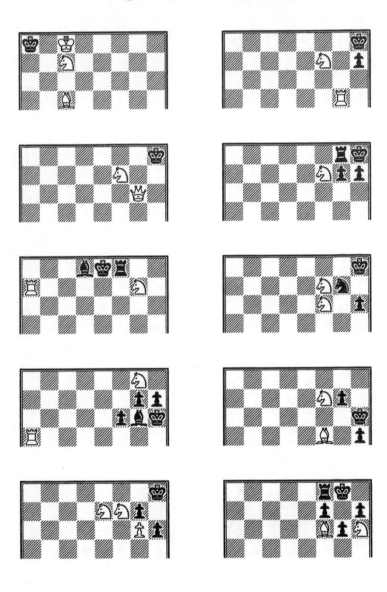

Knight Checkmates

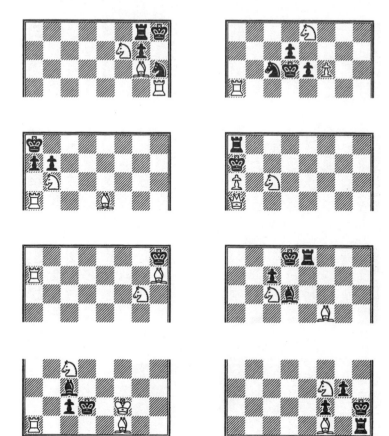

Pawn Checkmates

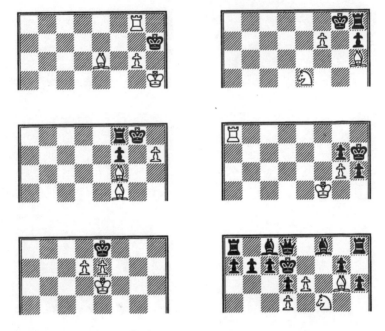

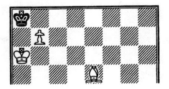

Stalemate is a Draw!

Stalemate is the name given to a position where the side to move does not have a legal move. The game cannot continue, but it is not checkmate. No one has won, so the result is a draw!

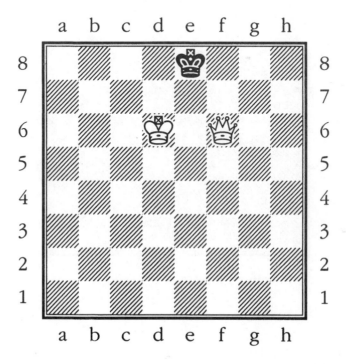

It is Black's move.

No matter where Black tries to go he will be in check, which is not allowed. But it is not checkmate because Black isn't even in check.

With Black to move it is stalemate, and the game is a draw. If Black had another piece in the diagram then it would not be stalemate as he could move that piece.

It is only stalemate when the side to move has no move at all which he is allowed to make.

Not Stalemate

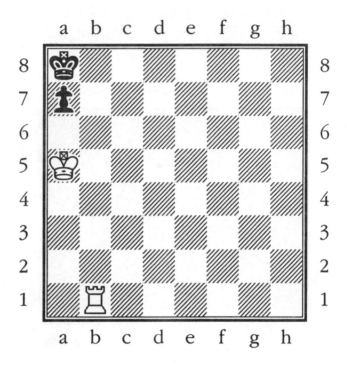

This is not stalemate because Black can move his pawn. After Black plays a6 it will be stalemate if White plays ♔xa6. So White should play a rook move or ♔b6.

Black to Move

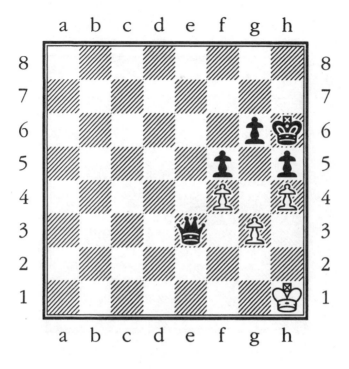

If Black plays ♕xg3 it is stalemate. Therefore he should bring his king right round the board to help his queen to checkmate the white king.

Another possibility for Black is to play ♕f2 when White can only move g4. Black could then continue ♕xh4+ followed by ♕xg4+.

White to Move

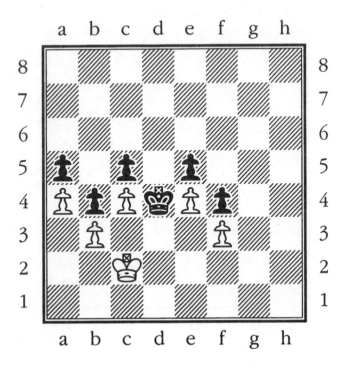

White should play ♔d2 and stalemate Black. Any other White move will let Black play ♚e3 and ♚xf3. In a few more moves Black will queen his f-pawn and win the game.

Perpetual Check

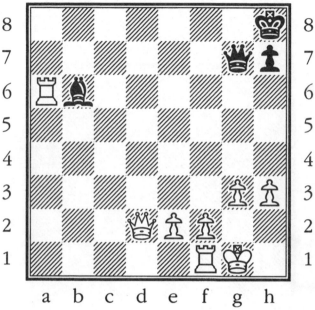

Black plays ♛xg3+. White must play ♔h1 because the f2 pawn is pinned. Black continues ♛xh3+ and White has to play ♔g1. Black now plays ♛g3+ and we are back where we started, so the players agree to a draw.

A game of chess is also drawn if:

1: the players agree a draw.

2: there are not enough pieces left to force checkmate, for example king against king; king and bishop against king; king and knight against king or king and two knights against king.

3: both players make fifty moves without taking anything or moving a pawn.

4: if the same position keeps occurring, as in the last two diagrams.

5: one player is stalemated.

Perpetual Check

This is another way to draw a game of chess. If you are losing the game then you can try to check the enemy king 'forever' (that is what 'perpetual' means).

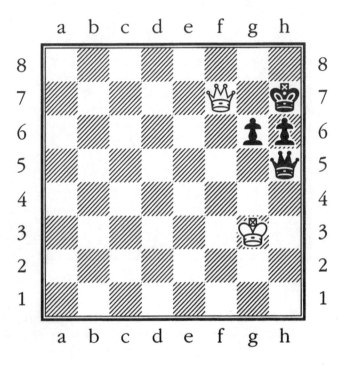

Black has two extra pawns and so is winning the game. White, looking for a way to draw, has played ♕f7+. This is the position in the diagram. Black can only play ♔h8. Then White can check again by ♕f8+ and Black can only play ♔h7. White then does it all over again by ♕f7+. There is no way that Black can avoid this, so he has to agree to a draw.

In all the little puzzles that follow (pages 87-115), *White plays up the board* and it is *White to move*. The headings to each page will give you an idea of what to look for. First try to work out the answers for yourself. If you cannot do that then do not worry, just look at the answer at the bottom of the page and work it out. The important thing is that you understand the answer.

Checkmate in One Move

In all the positions that follow, it is White to move and White is moving UP the board.

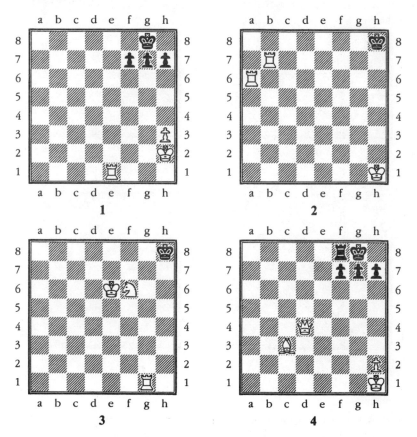

1 **2**

3 **4**

Answers

1: ♖e8 mate

2: ♖a8 mate

3: ♖g8 mate. If ♖h1+, Black can play ♚g7.

4: ♕xg7 mate

Checkmate in One Move

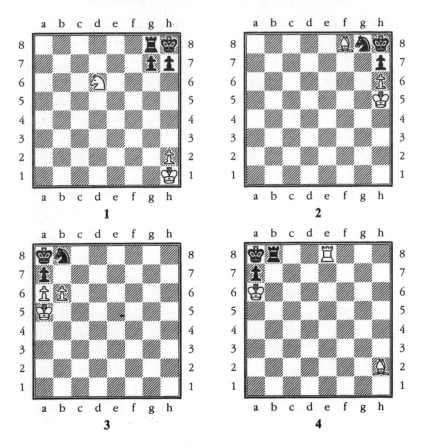

1

2

3

4

Answers

1: ♘f7 mate

2: ♗g7 mate

3: b7 mate

4: ♖xb8 mate. ♗xb8 is stalemate—a draw!

Checkmate in One Move

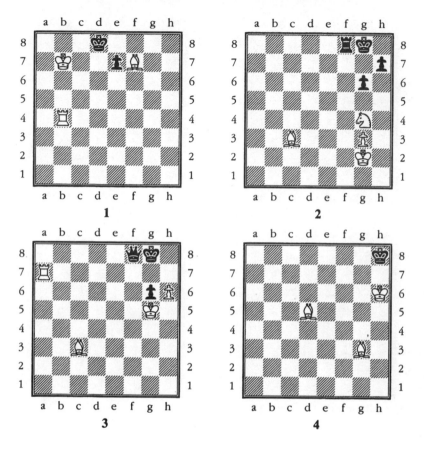

Answers

1: ♖d4 mate

2: ♘h6 mate

3: h7 mate

4: ♗e5 mate

Checkmate in One Move

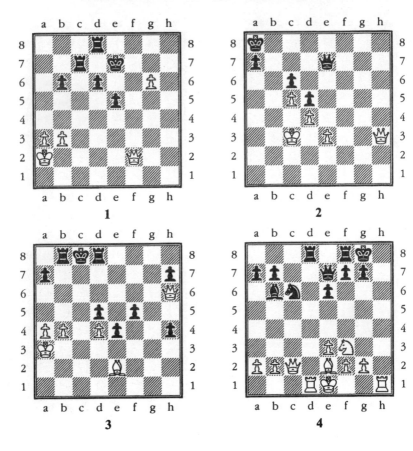

Answers

1: ♕f7 mate

2: ♕c8 mate

3: ♕c6 mate

4: ♕h7 mate

Checkmate in One Move

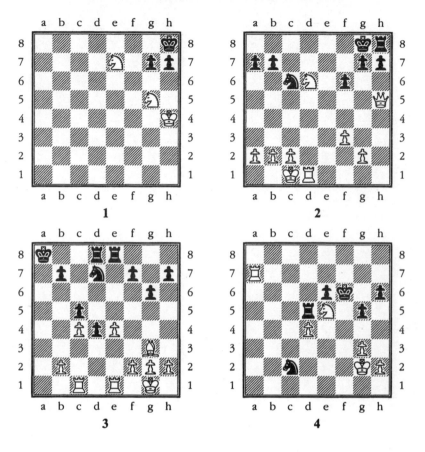

Answers

1: ♘f7 mate

2: ♕f7 mate or ♕e8 mate. There is a mate in two moves by 1 ♕d5+ ♚f8 2 ♕f7 mate.

3: ♖a1 mate

4: ♖f7 mate

Checkmate in One Move

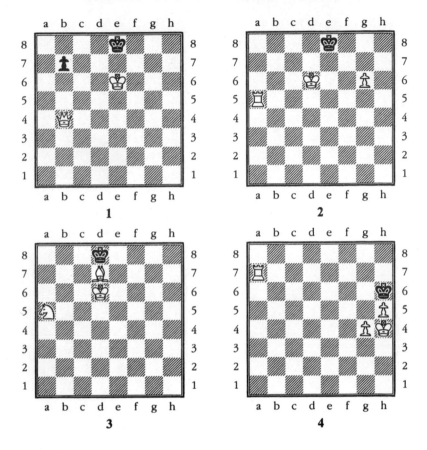

1

2

3

4

Answers

1: ♛e7 mate

2: ♖a8 mate

3: ♘b7 mate or ♘c6 mate

4: g5 mate

Checkmate by Pawn Promotion

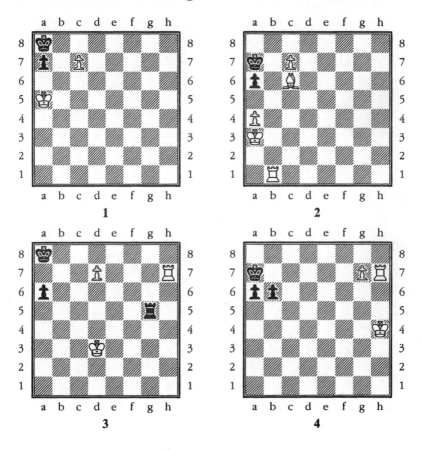

1

2

3

4

Answers

1: c8=♕ mate

2: c8=♘ mate

3: d8=♕ mate or d8=♖ mate

4: g8=♕ mate or g8=♖ mate

Checkmate by Pawn Promotion

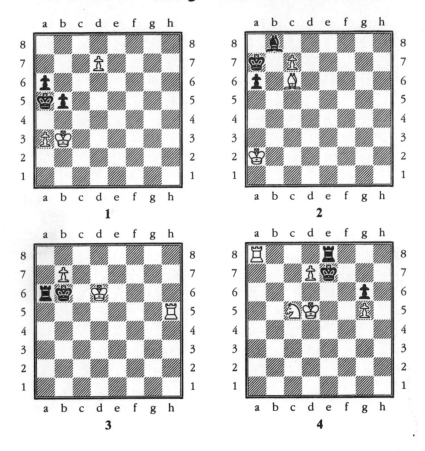

Answers

1: d8=♕ mate or d8=♗ mate

2: c8=♘ mate (if cxb8=♕+ Black plays ♔xb8)

3: b8=♕ mate

4: dxe8=♕ mate

Checkmate using a Pin

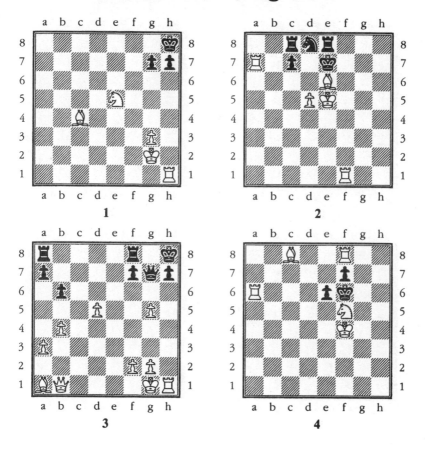

1

2

3

4

Answers

1: ♘g6 mate. Not 1 ♘f7+ ♔g8.

2: d6 mate. The pawn on c7 is pnned.

3: ♕xh7 mate. The black queen is pinned.

4: ♖xe6 mate. The f7 pawn is pinned.

Checkmate using a Pin

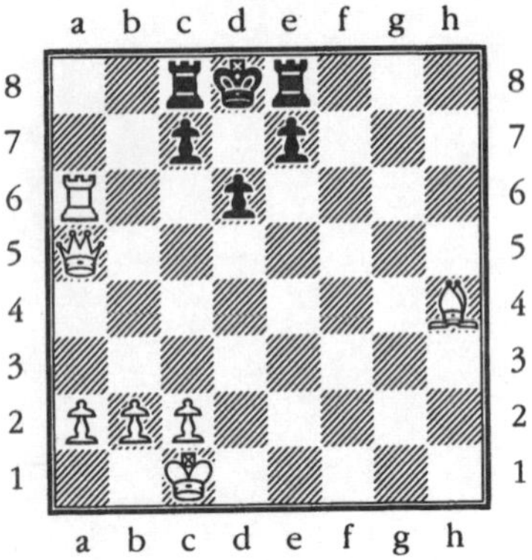

1

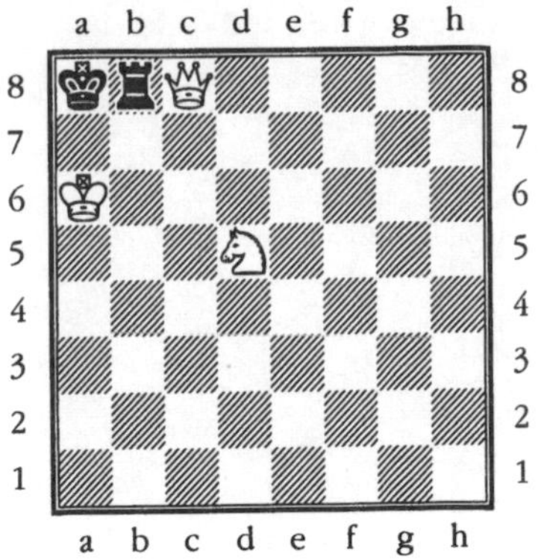

2

3

4

Answers

1: ♖xd6 mate. The other black pawns are both pinned.

2: ♘b6 mate or ♘c7 mate

3: ♖d8 mate. The black knight is pinned by the white pawn.

4: ♘xf7 mate

Checkmate using a Pin

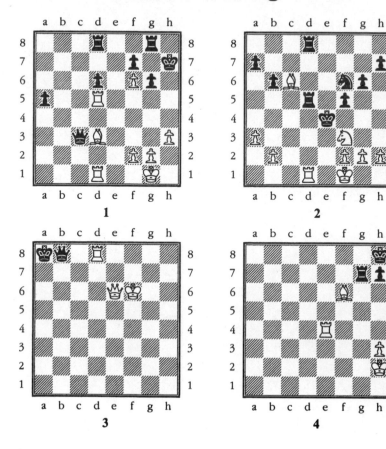

1

2

3

4

Answers

1: ♖h5 mate

2: ♖d4 mate

3: ♕a6 mate

4: ♖e8 mate

Checkmate using a Pin

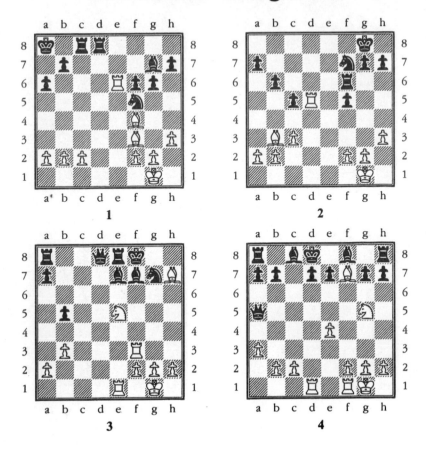

1

2

3

4

Answers

1: ♖xa6 mate

2: ♖d8 mate. Now the bishop pins the knight.

3: ♘g6 mate or ♖xf7 mate

4: ♘e6 mate

Various Checkmates in One Move

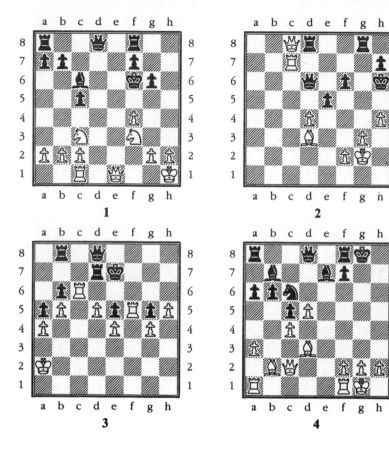

1

2

3

4

Answers

1: ♕e5 mate

2: ♖xh7 mate

3: ♖e6 mate

4: ♗h7 mate

Various Checkmates in One Move

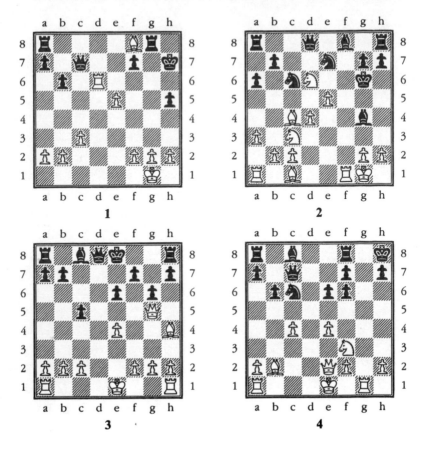

Answers

1: ♖h6 mate

2: ♗f7 mate

3: ♛xd8 mate

4: ♗xf6 mate

Various Checkmates in One Move

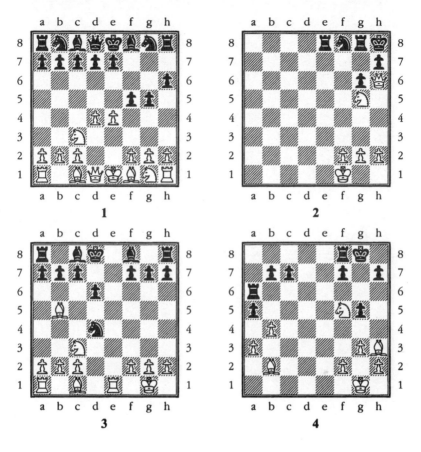

1

2

3

4

Answers

1: ♕h5 mate

2: ♘f7 mate

3: ♖e8 mate

4: ♘e7 mate. Not 1 ♘h6+ ♖xh6.

101

Various Checkmates in One Move

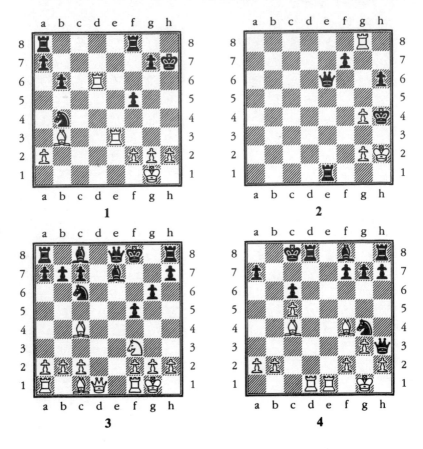

1

2

3

4

Answers

1: ♖h3 mate

2: g3 mate

3: ♗h6 mate

4: ♗a6 mate

Various Checkmates in One Move

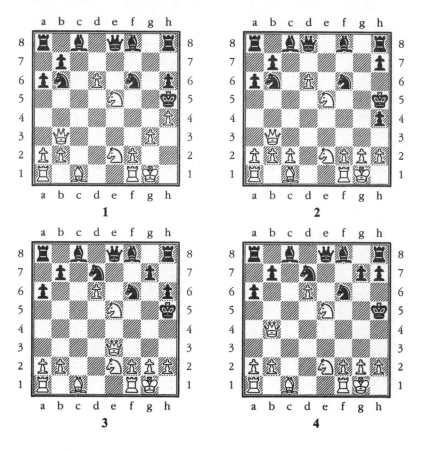

1

2

3

4

Now, 8 very similar positions. Think carefully!

Answers

1: ♘f4 mate. If 1 ♕f3+ then ♗g4 or ♘g4 blocks the check.

2: ♕f7 mate. If 1 ♘f4+ ♔g5 or ♔h6.

3: ♕h3 mate

4: ♘g3 mate

Various Checkmates in One Move

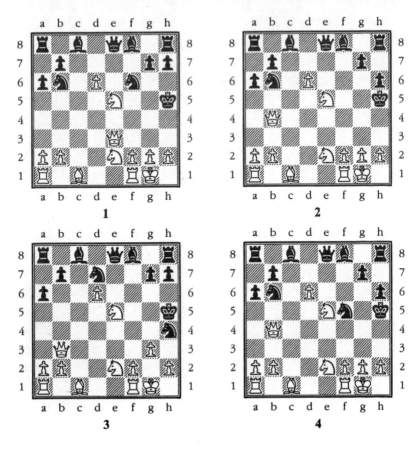

1

2

3

4

Answers

1: ♕g5 mate

2: ♘g3 mate

3: g4 mate

4: ♕g4 mate. If 1 ♘f4+ ♚g5 or 1 ♘g3+ ♘xg3.

Various Checkmates in One Move

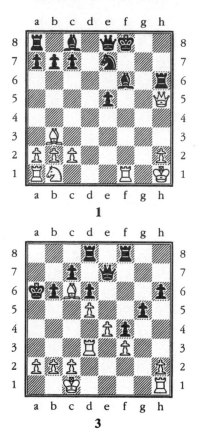

1

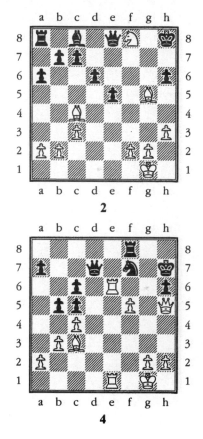

2

3

4

Answers

1: ♕xh6 mate

2: ♗f6 mate

3: ♖a3 mate

4: ♕g6 mate

Various Checkmates in One Move

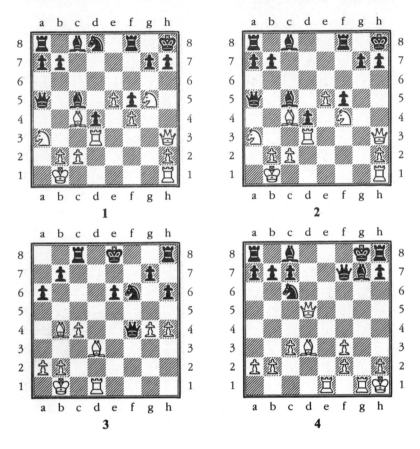

1

2

3

4

Answers

1: ♛xh7 mate

2: ♘g6 mate. The h-pawn is pinned.

3: ♝g6 mate. The white rook prevents ♚d7 or ♚d8.

4: ♜e8 mate. The black queen is pinned.

Various Checkmates in One Move

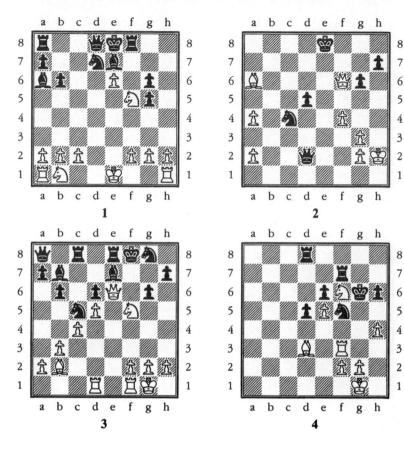

1

2

3

4

Answers

1: ♘g7 mate

2: ♗b5 mate

3: ♗g7 mate

4: ♖g3 mate. The black knght is pinned.

Various Checkmates in One Move

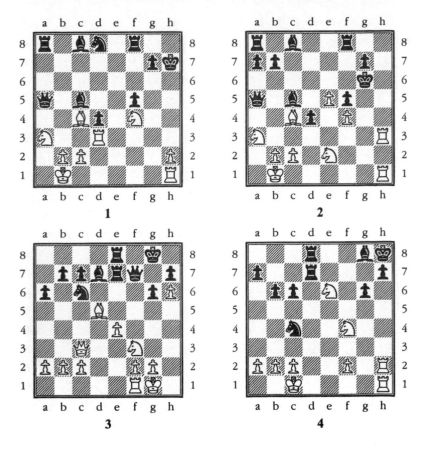

1

2

3

4

Answers

1: ♖h3 mate

2: ♖g1 mate or ♖g3 mate

3: ♕g7 mate. The black queen is pinned.

4: ♘xg6 mate. The h-pawn is pinned.

Various Checkmates in One Move

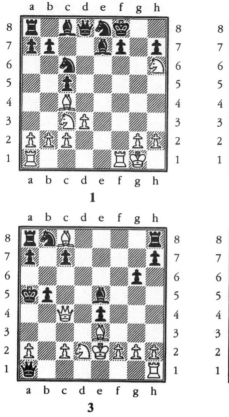

1

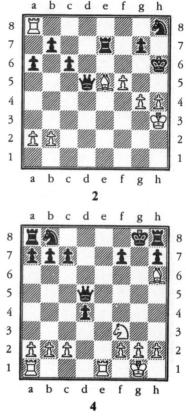

2

3

4

Answers

1:   Rxf7 mate

2:   Rxh8 mate

3:   Nb3 mate

4:   Re8 mate

Various Checkmates in One Move

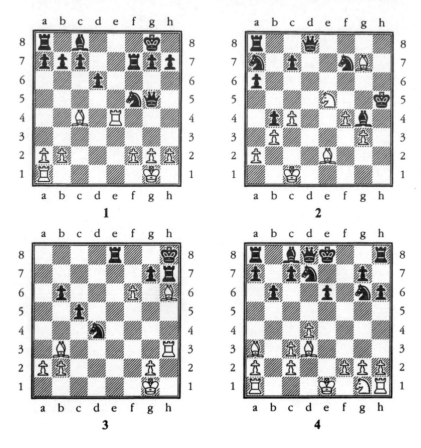

1

2

3

4

Answers

1: ♖e8 mate

2: ♗xg4 mate

3: ♗xg7 mate. The black rook on h7 is now pinned.

4: ♗xg6 mate

110

Mates by Discovered and Double Check

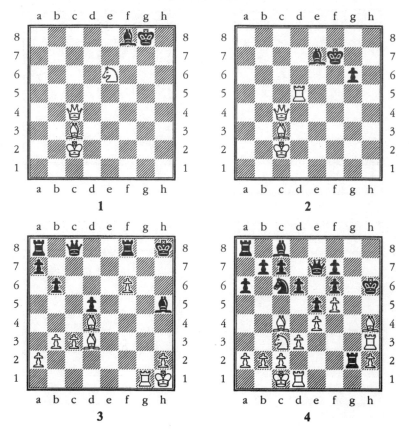

1

2

3

4

Answers

1: ♘g5 mate—the only knight move that prevents ♚h7.

2: ♖d8 mate—only this rook move prevents ♚e8 and ♚f8.

3: f7 mate

4: ♗xf6 mate—the bishop stops ♚g7.

Mates by Discovered and Double Check

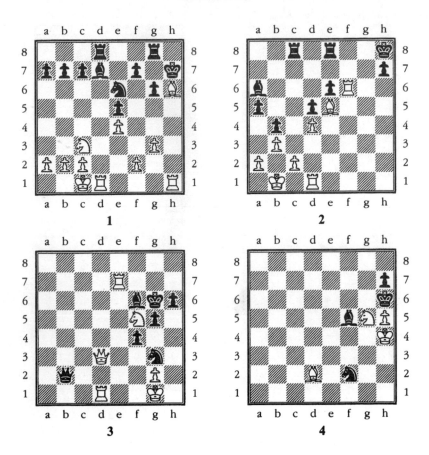

1

2

3

4

Answers

1: ♗f8 mate

2: ♜f8 mate or ♜g6 mate

3: ♘xg3 mate—preventing ♔h5.

4: ♘e6 mate—the knight prevents ♔g7.

Mates by Discovered and Double Check

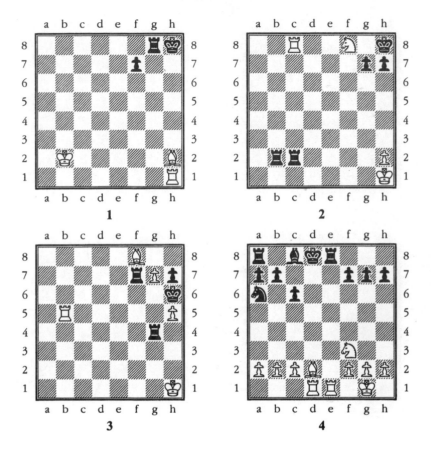

1

2

3

4

Answers

1: ♗e5 mate—double check.

2: ♘g6 mate—double check

3: g8=♘ mate—double check. Other promotions allow ♖g7.

4: ♗a5 mate—double check.

Mates by Discovered and Double Check

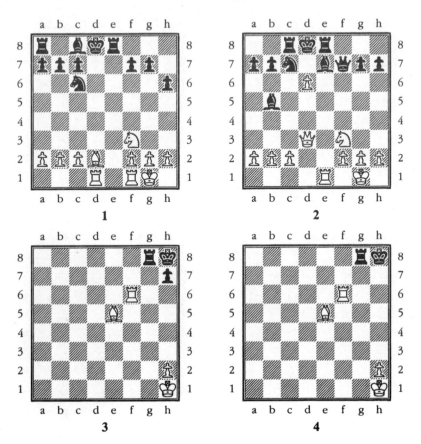

1

2

3

4

Answers

1: ♗g5 mate

2: dxe7 mate. Not 1 dxc7+ ♔xc7.

3: ♖f8 mate

4: ♖h6 mate

Mates by Discovered and Double Check

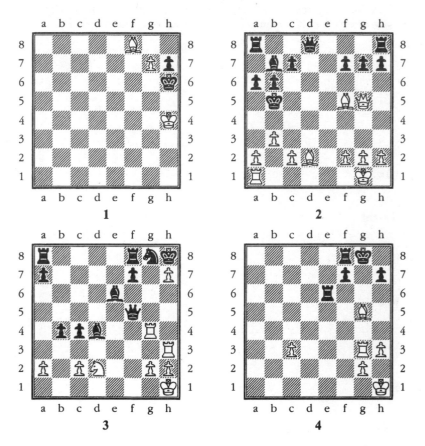

1

2

3

4

Answers

1: g8=♕ mate or g8=♖ mate

2: ♗d7 mate. 1 ♗d3+ ♔c6.

3: hxg8=♕ mate or hxg8=♖ mate

4: ♗f6 mate

What are the Pieces Worth?

The value of a piece depends upon how many squares it attacks. The more squares it can attack simultaneously, the more powerful it is.

Look at this table:

	Fewest squares it can attack	Most squares it can attack
Pawn	1	2
Knight	2	8
Bishop	7	13
Rook	14	14
Queen	21	27
King	3	8

These figures are correct for an empty board.

See if you can find the positions on the board where each piece has its greatest and fewest number of attacked squares. The diagrams on the next page will help.

What are the Pieces Worth?

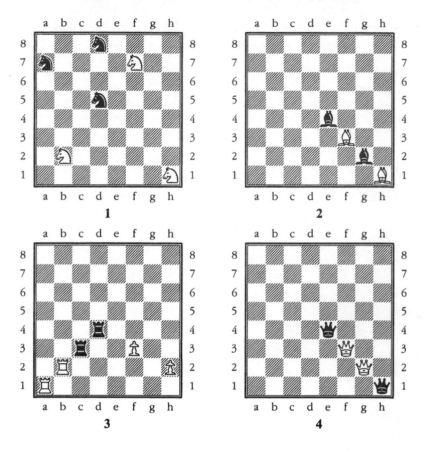

1

2

3

4

How many squares do each of these pieces attack if there are no other pieces on the board?

What are the Pieces Worth?

The nearer a piece gets to the centre of the board the stronger it gets (apart from the rook).

If you look at the tables on page 98 and this page, the knight seems to be given too much value. This is because in actual play there are many pieces on the board and these pieces usually block the lines that the bishops, rooks and queens move along. The knight is almost never blocked so it is worth more than it seems.

The bishop is worth less than you expect. This is because it can only move on squares of one colour. Two bishops together are very powerful if not blocked.

Remember that the values of pieces change during a game, usually only by a little but sometimes a lot. On the next page are some diagrams showing pieces in very bad positions and so worth very little.

♙	**1**	♟
♘	**3¼**	♞
♗	**3½**	♝
♖	**5**	♜
♕	**9**	♛
♔	**no attacking value**	♚

Examples of Weak Pieces

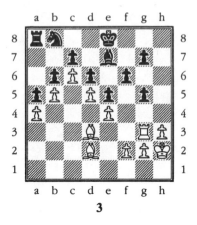

1

2

The white bishops in these two positions have very little power. White will be lucky not to lose.

3

Black has three pieces and they have only three safe moves between them!

The word 'pieces' is used in two different ways in chess. Sometimes it means all the chessmen and sometimes it means only the strong chessmen—not the pawns.

Examples of Strong Pieces

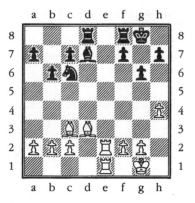

The white bishops cut across the open board and right through the black king's position.

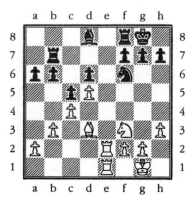

The white rooks control the e-file and Black will be lucky to prevent White from playing ♖e7 or ♖e8 in the near future.

For the rest of this book we will count bishops and knights as about equal in value, but it is important to know that sometimes they are not!

Attacking and Defending Pieces

One way to win a game of chess is to set about winning your opponent's pieces so that you will have more pieces with which to attack and checkmate his king.

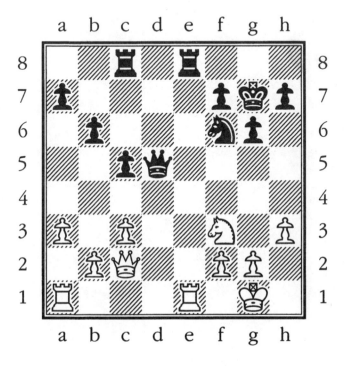

If White plays ♖a1-d1 (♖ad1 for short) he attacks the black queen which will have to retreat because the queen is too valuable to lose.

Instead White might play ♖xe8 when Black will reply either ♖xe8 or ♘xe8 and they will have 'exchanged' rooks.

Attacking and Defending Pieces

In each position find a move for White where a less valuable piece attacks a more valuable one, forcing it to move. Look for a way to do this which will not give a piece away. The answers are under the diagrams.

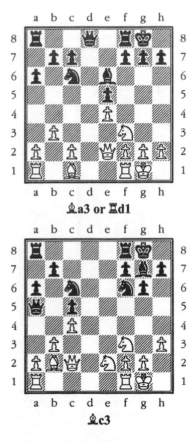

♗a3 or ♖d1

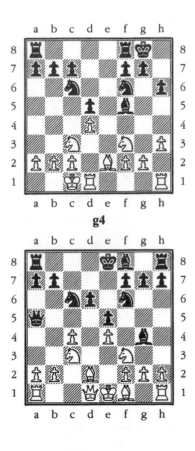

g4

♗c3

b4 attacks the black queen but the pawn can be taken in three different ways.

(1) ♘ **on c3 anywhere** and the bishop attacks the queen or (2) **h3** attacking the bishop.

Attacking and Defending Pieces

If a piece attacks an enemy piece of the same or lower value, the enemy's piece can move or be defended.

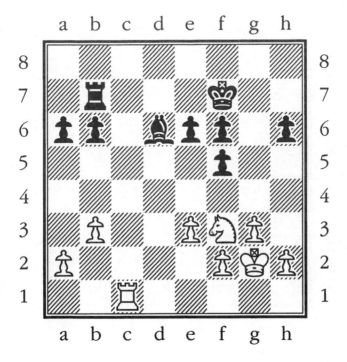

White plays ♖c6 attacking the bishop. Black can move the bishop or defend it by ♔e7 so that if White plays ♖xd6 he can reply ♔xd6 winning a rook for a bishop. Black could defend the bishop by ♖d7 but that allows ♖xb6.

Attacking and Defending Pieces

The knight on f7 is attacked by White. How can Black defend the piece safely?

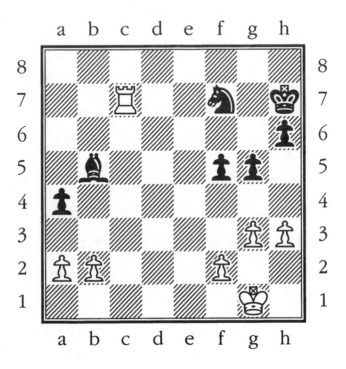

♚g8, ♚g7, ♚g6 or ♝e8. Not ♝c4 because of ♖xc4. Of the king moves ♚g7 is worst because it leaves the knight pinned and a pinned piece has no power. ♚g8 takes the king away from his pawns and the king is a good defender of pawns. If ♝e8, White plays ♖e7 and he will win either the bishop or the knight. So Black's best move is ♚g6.

Attacking and Defending Pieces

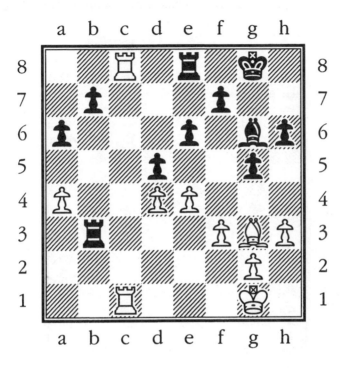

The rook on e8 is attacked. Black can defend the rook by ♔f8 or by f6 or f5 (defending with the bishop). There is another way to 'defend' the rook, by playing ♖f8.

Black could also play ♖xc8, exchanging rooks but this would put the second white rook in a good position.

Attacking and Defending Pieces

White's bishop on f1 attacks the undefended black bishop on c4.

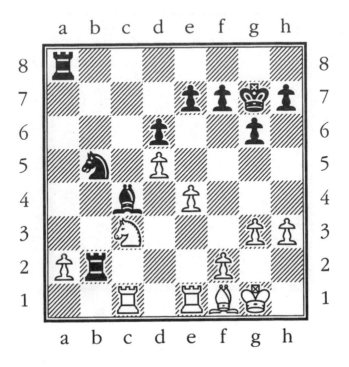

The bishop on c4 can be defended by ♖c8, ♖b4 or ♘a3. Instead of defending the bishop, Black could play the exchange ♝xf1.

♝xa2 would be bad because Black would lose the knight on b5. It would be attacked twice by the knight and the bishop and only defended once.

Black could defend his bishop by ♖a4 but White would reply ♘xa4.

Attacking and Defending Pieces

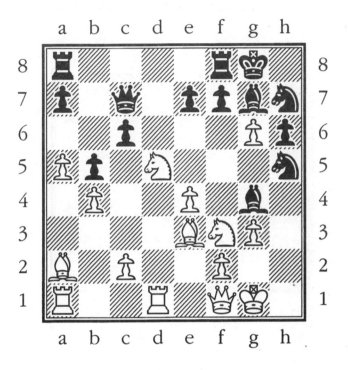

This is a very complicated position.

1: How many pieces are both undefended and attacked?
Only the ♛ on c7, ♞ on f3 and pawn on g6.

2: How many things are attacked by something of lower value?
♛c7, ♞h7, ♞d5, ♖a1. The most important of these is the ♛c7 so if Black is to move he will save his queen and the best way is to capture its attacker by cxd5.

If it is White to move he will take the queen by ♞xc7 but first he will play gxh7+ because Black must get out of check and White will still be able to play ♞xc7 next move.

Attacking and Defending Pieces

1: Which pieces are both attacked and undefended?

♖c8, ♘e3, ♘h3, and the pawns on a7, c3 and c5.

2: Which pieces are attacked by ones of lower value?

Did you notice that White was in check? The queen on f6 and rook on f2 are also attacked.

3: How can White get out of check?

♖xe3, ♔xh3, ♔g3 or ♔h1.

Take for Nothing

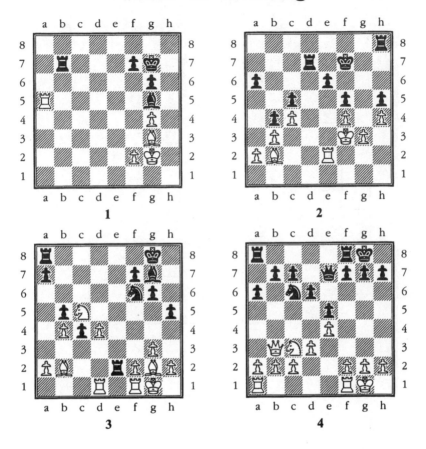

Answers

1: 1 ♖xg5

2: 1 ♗xh8

3: 1 ♗xa8

4: 1 ♕xb7

Take a More Important Piece

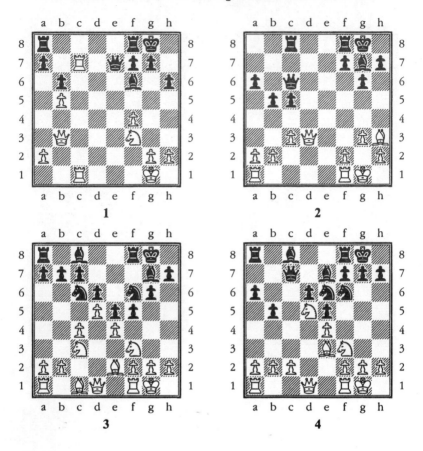

Answers

1: 1 ♖xe7 wins queen for rook.

2: 1 ♗xc8 wins rook for bishop (the exchange).

3: 1 dxc6 wins knight for pawn.

4: 1 ♘xc7 wins queen for knight.

First Way to Defend

If your opponent attacks one of your pieces, what do you do? You must answer the question—if he takes my piece, will he gain? Look to see if your piece is defended and whether the attacker is less valuable or more valuable than your piece.

If the attacker is less valuable then you must move your piece but if it is of equal value or more valuable then you can either defend your piece or move it.

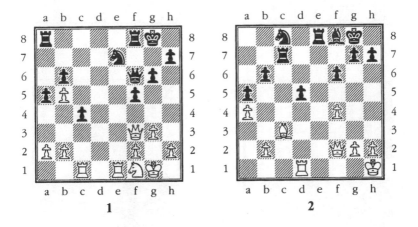

1   2

Answers

1: White cannot take the rook on a8 because he would lose his queen. Nor can he take the knight on e7 because he would lose his rook. In both cases the piece he loses is worth more than the one he takes. However, White can play ♖xc4 because the pawn is not defended.

2: 1 ♕xb6? loses the queen to 1...♘xb6. 1 ♗xa5? and 1 ♗xf6? both lose the bishop because the black pawns are both guarded. White knows that Black is unlikely to play ♖xc3 because after bxc3 Black has lost the exchange (rook for bishop). 1 ♖xd5 wins a pawn.

Move or Defend

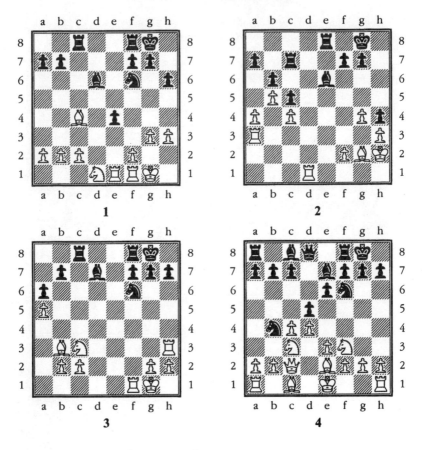

Answers

1: Black threatens ♖xc4. The bishop can be defended by b3 or ♘e3 or moved to b3. If the bishop goes to e2 or b5, Black can play ♖xc2. If it goes anywhere else, Black can take the bishop.

2: Black threatens ♗xc4. White can only defend this pawn, not move it. The possible moves are ♖c3, ♖c1, ♗f1 or ♗d5.

3: Black threatens ♗xh3. Because the rook is more valuable than the bishop, White must move it to h4, g3, f3, e3 or d3.

4: Black threatens ♘xc2+ so White must move his queen. There are five safe squares—find them!

More Attackers

One important and quite common way to win enemy pieces is to attack them more times than they are defended and then just take them.

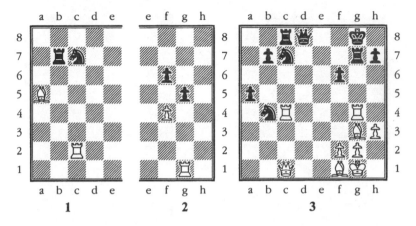

1: The black knight is attacked twice and only defended once. White can win it by playing ♗xc7 or ♖xc7.

2: The black pawn on g5 is also attacked twice and defended only once so 1 fxg5 wins a pawn because if Black plays 1...fxg5 then 2 ♖xg5.

3: This is more complicated because it is important that you do a little more than just count the number of attackers and defenders. For example, the knight on b4 is attacked twice and only defended once but 1 ♖xb4? axb4 2 ♖xb4 only wins a knight and a pawn for a rook, which is not enough. If the pawn on a5 is turned into a bishop then the same moves would win two pieces for the rook. Now look at the other black knight, on c7. It is attacked three times by the white bishop, rook on c4 AND by the white queen (because after the rook on c4 takes on c7 the queen's attack on that square will be real). Black seems to defend the knight on c7 three times so it looks safe. However, one of the 'defenders' is the rook on g7 which is pinned! A pinned piece cannot usually act as a defender. 1 ♖xc7! wins a knight (1...♖xc7 2 ♕xc7 ♕xc7 3 ♗xc7). 1 ♗xc7! also wins the knight. If you are not very happy about doing things this way round, then play 1 ♖xg7+ and after 1...♔xg7 then you can play 2 ♖xc7 because you really do have an extra attacker now!

More Attackers

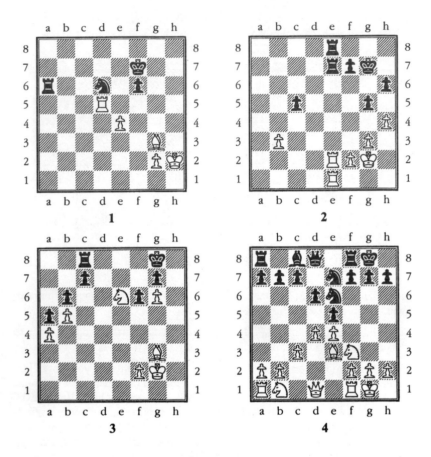

Answers

1: 1 ♖xd6 wins a knight and so does 1 ♗xd6. The knight was attacked twice and only defended once.

2: The rook on e7 is attacked twice. 1 ♖xe7 wins a rook.

3: White can win the pawn on c7. He just takes it with either his knight or bishop.

4: The black pawn on e5 is attacked by the pawn on d4 and knight on f3, so 1 dxe5 and if 1...dxe5 then 2 ♘xe5.

134

Another Kind of Pin

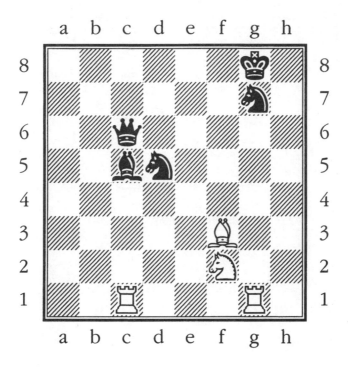

You already know that the rook on g1 pins the black knight on g7 which is *not allowed* to move in this position.

The other black knight is also pinned, by the white bishop on f3. The knight is *allowed* to move but if it does the white bishop will take the valuable black queen.

There are two other pins shown in the diagram, but the pin by the black bishop on the white knight is not important at the moment because the black bishop is itself pinned.

Another Kind of Pin

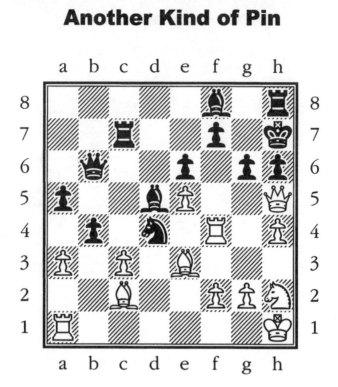

1 How many pieces are pinned against one of the kings?

The pawns on g6, h6 and g2.

2 How many other pins can you find?

The pawn on c3 because the ♗c2 is undefended. The ♘d4 is pinned by the bishop on e3.

Pins

The diagrams on pages 138-146 show White winning by using a pin. There are three main types of pin:-

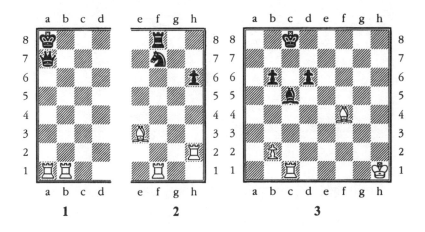

1   **2**   **3**

1: The rook on a1 pins the queen against the king. The queen is lost (for a rook). Provided the piece which pins is worth less than the pinned piece, this method wins material. See diagrams on pages 138-139.

2: The knight cannot move because of ♖xf8—it is pinned. White cannot play ♖xf7 because after Black replies ♖xf7, White has lost rook for knight (the exchange). So White attacks the knight again by ♖hf2! Now White wins the knight for nothing! See diagrams on pages 140-143.

3: The black bishop cannot move—it is pinned. This means that it is not defending the black pawns so ♗xd6 wins a pawn. See diagrams on pages 144-146. By attacking the bishop again White can win it. Because the bishop is defended, it needs to be attacked by something worth less. 1 b4! wins the bishop for a pawn.

In diagram 2, 1 ♗xh6 wins a pawn (1...♘xh6? 2 ♖xf8). A pinned piece does not defend.

Pin a Major Piece

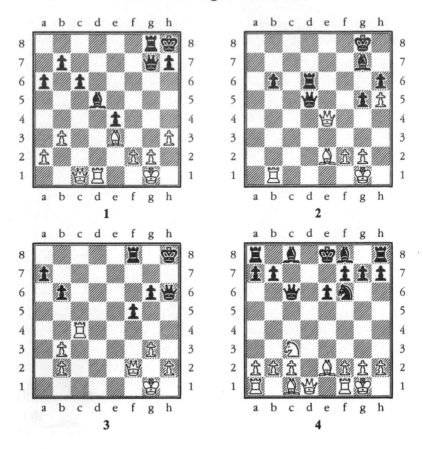

1

2

3

4

Answers

1: 1 ♗d4 wins the queen.

2: 1 ♗c4. If 1...♕xc4 then 2 ♕xc4+ and Black's queen is lost.

3: 1 ♖h4

4: 1 ♗b5

Pin a Major Piece

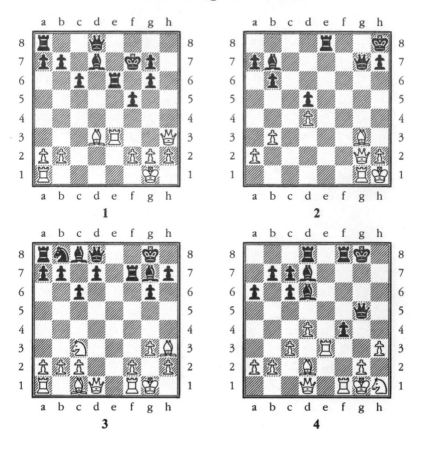

1

2

3

4

Answers

1: 1 ♗c4 wins the exchange (rook for bishop).

2: 1 ♗e5 pins the queen and attacks it three times!

3: 1 ♗e6 wins the exchange because 1...dxe6?? loses the queen to 2 ♕xd8+.

4: 1 ♖g3 because the white bishop pins the f-pawn and if 1...♕xg3 then 2 ♘xg3.

Attack a Pinned Piece

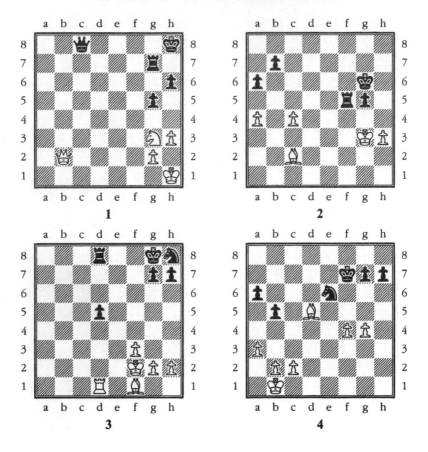

Answers

1: 1 ♘h5! (not 1 ♘f5?? ♛xf5).

2: 1 ♔g4! wins a whole rook.

3: 1 ♗c4! wins a pawn. Also possible is 1 ♖xd5! ♖xd5 2 ♗c4! getting the rook back.

4: 1 f5!

Attack a Pinned Piece

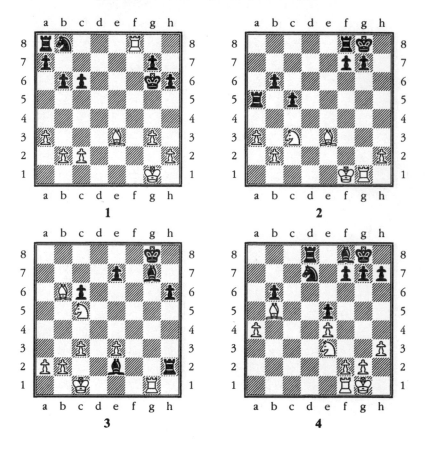

1

2

3

4

Answers

1: 1 ♗f4 wins a knight.

2: 1 ♗h6! wins the g-pawn which is pinned in two different ways.

3: 1 ♘e6 wins the bishop on g7.

4: 1 ♖d1.

Attack a Pinned Piece

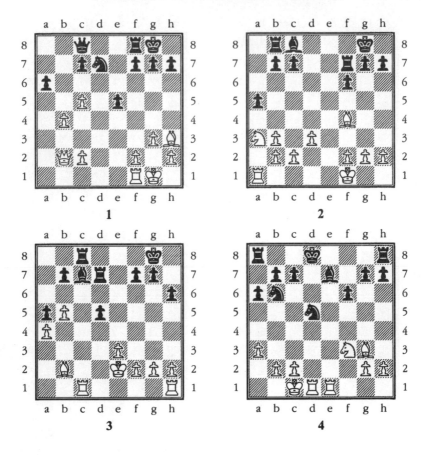

1

2

3

4

Answers

1: 1 c6! is best but 1 ♖d1 is also possible. Usually it is best to attack with the less valuable piece.

2: 1 ♘b5 wins the pawn on c7.

3: 1 ♗e5 works in the end but the best move is 1 b6! which wins a piece immediately.

4: 1 c4 wins a knight. 1...♘xc4 2 ♖xd5+.

Attack a Pinned Piece

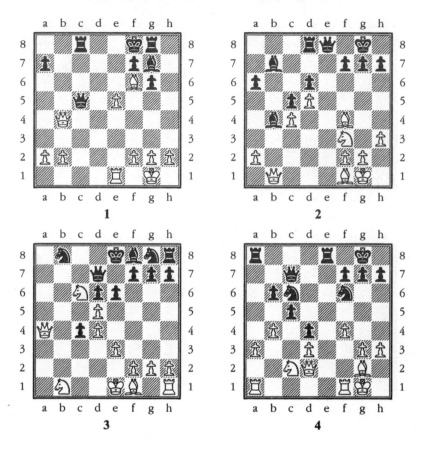

1

2

3

4

Answers

1: 1 ♖c1! wins the pinned queen because if 1...♛xb4? 2 ♖xc8 is mate!

2: 1 a3 and White will win one of the bishops.

3: The white knight on c6 is pinned but it attacks the undefended knight on b8. 1 ♛a8! breaks the pin, pins the black knight and wins it.

4: 1 b5 attacks the pinned knight. Black should move the knight and only lose the exchange.

A Pinned Piece does not defend

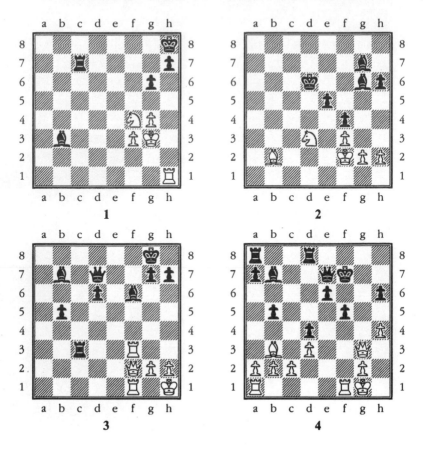

1

2

3

4

Answers

1: 1 ♘xg6+ wns a pawn.

2: Black threatens ♗xd3. 1 ♘xf4! wins a pawn.

3: 1 ♖xc3! wins a rook (1...♗xc3?? 2 ♕f8 mate!).

4: 1 ♖xf5+!

A Pinned Piece does not defend

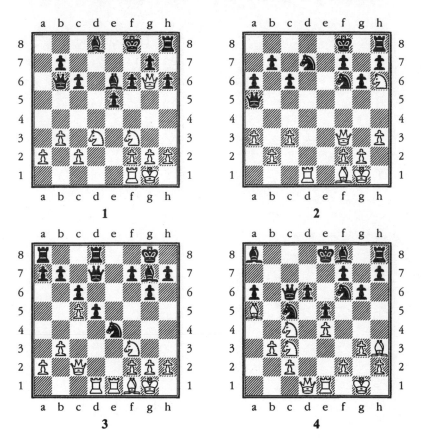

1

2

3

4

Answers

1: 1 ♘dxe5 or 1 ♘fxe5 wins a pawn—1...fxe5 2 ♕xe6.

2: 1 ♖xd7! wins a knight—1...♘xd7?? 2 ♕xf7 mate!

3: 1 ♖xe4!

4: 1 ♘xe5! because if 1...dxe5 2 ♕d8 mate!

A Pinned Piece does not defend

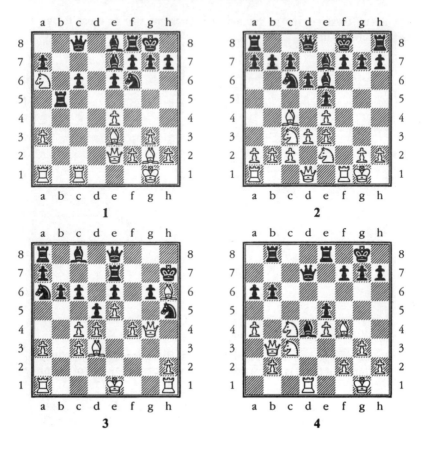

1

2

3

4

Answers

1: 1 ♕xb5 wins a rook (1...cxb5 2 ♖xc8).

2: 1 ♗xe6

3: 1 ♕xh5 gets his piece back and defends his bishop.

4: 1 ♘xe5 or 1 ♗xe5. The pawn defended the bishop but the bishop didn't defend the pawn!

Queen Forks

A queen fork is a queen move which threatens two or more things at once. There are three types:-

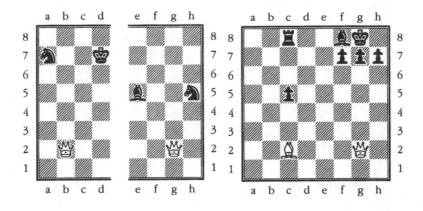

1: 1 ♕b7+ or ♕d4+ both fork the king and knight. The king must move and White plays ♕xa7. See diagrams on pages 148-151.

2: 1 ♕e2 or ♕g5 both fork the black pieces. Black is not forced to play anything but there is no way to prevent White winning one of the pieces next move. See diagrams on pages 152-154.

3: White plays 1 ♕h3 which threatens ♕xh7 mate and ♕xc8—a fork! Black must stop the mate (by something like g6) and White wins the rook. See diagrams on pages 155-157.

Look for undefended black pieces.

Queen Forks with Check

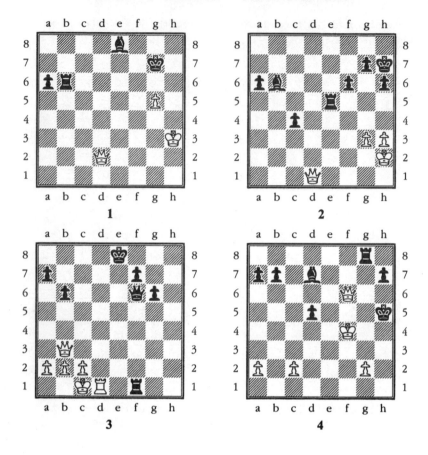

Answers

1: 1 ♕d4+ wins the rook.

2: 1 ♕b1+ wins the bishop.

3: 1 ♕b5+ wins the rook because it is now attacked twice.

4: 1 ♕f7+ forks king, rook, bishop and pawns!

Queen Forks with Check

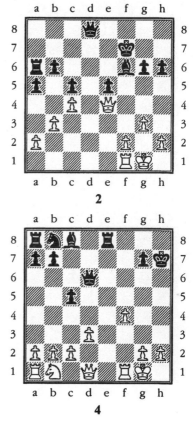

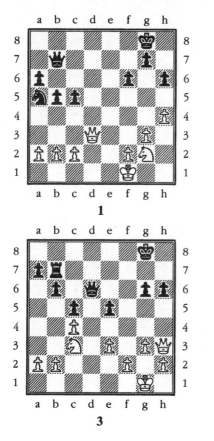

Answers

1: 1 ♛d8+ wins the knight.

2: 1 ♛b7+ wins the rook.

3: 1 ♛c8+ wins the rook.

4: 1 ♛h5+ wins the rook.

Queen Forks with Check

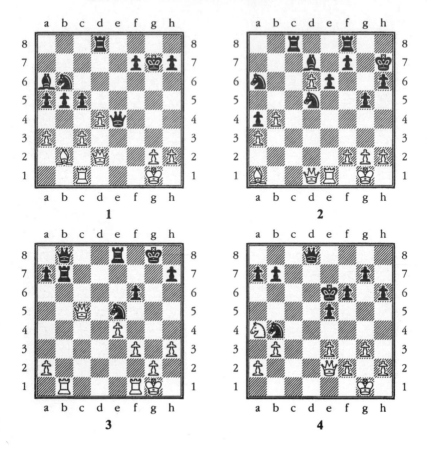

Answers

1: 1 ♕g5+ wins the rook.

2: 1 ♕d3+ wins the knight on a6.

3: 1 ♕d5+ wins the rook on b7 because it is now attacked twice, and if 1...♖f7 then 2 ♖xb8.

4: 1 ♕g4+ is the easiest way to win the knight but 1 ♕c4+ ♘d5 2 e4 also works.

Queen Forks with Check

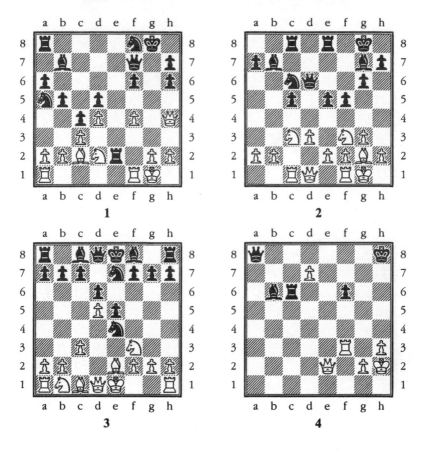

1

2

3

4

Answers

1: 1 ♛g4+ wins the rook on e2.

2: 1 ♛b3+ wins the bishop on b7.

3: 1 ♛a4+ wins the knight on e4.

4: 1 ♛e8+ ♛xe8 (or else Black loses his queen) 1 dxe8=♛+ and White has, in a way, won a queen! He also ends up by forking king and rook!

Queen Forks without Check

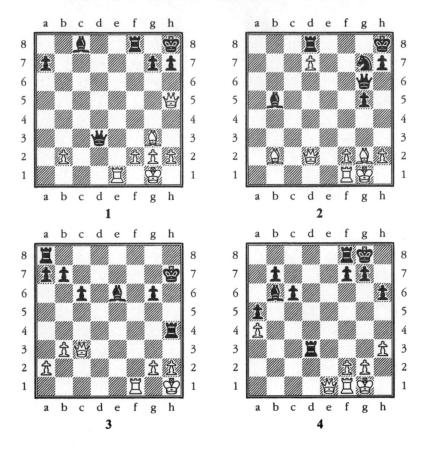

1

2

3

4

Answers

1: 1 ♕c5 forks rook and pawn on a7 and the rook must continue to protect the bishop so 1...♖f7 isn't possible.

2: 1 ♕a5 forks rook and bishop. 1...♗xf1 2 ♕xd8+ wins easily.

3: 1 ♕e1! forks the rook on h4 and bishop. 1 ♕f6? allows Black to defend by 1...♖e4!

4: 1 ♕b1! forks rook and bishop.

Queen Forks without Check

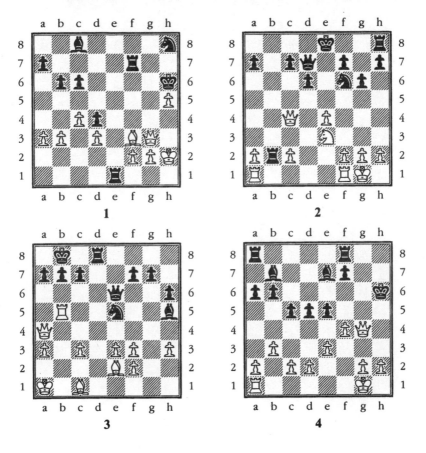

1

2

3

4

Answers

1: 1 ♕g8 forks bishop and knight.

2: 1 ♕c3 or 1 ♕d4 forks rook and knight.

3: 1 ♕h4 forks bishop and rook.

4: 1 ♕d7 forks the bishops.

Queen Forks without Check

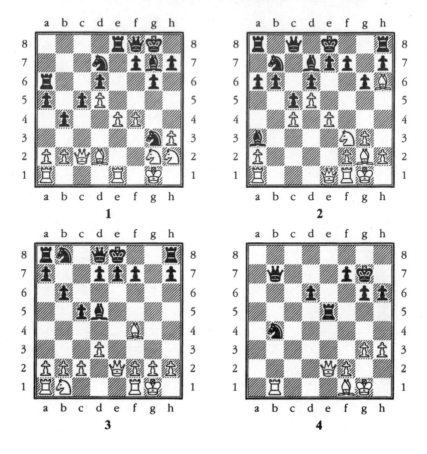

Answers

1: 1 ♕d3 forks the knight on g3 and rook on a6.

2: 1 ♕c3 forks bishop and rook.

3: 1 ♕e5 also forks bishop and rook.

4: White's queen is attacked. 1 ♕b2 wins the knight because it cannot be defended again (the rook is pinned!) but White also threatens f4 winning the rook!

Queen Fork with Mate Threat

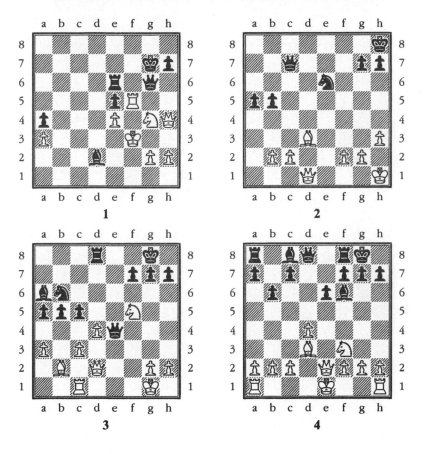

1

2

3

4

Answers

1: 1 ♕d8! threatens ♕xd2 and ♕f8 mate.

2: 1 ♕h5! wins the pawn on b5 because of the threats ♕xh7 mate and ♕e8+.

3: 1 ♕g5! attacks the rook and threatens ♕xg7 mate.

4: 1 ♕e4! wins the rook on a8 because Black must defend against ♕xh7 mate.

Queen Fork with Mate Threat

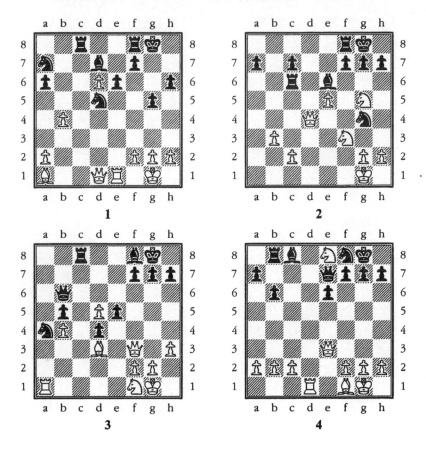

1

2

3

4

Answers

1: 1 ♕d4 threatens ♕xa7 and ♕g7 mate or ♕h8 mate.

2: 1 ♕e4 threatens ♕xc6 and ♕xh7 mate.

3: 1 ♕f5 threatens ♕xc8 and ♕xh7 mate.

4: 1 ♕g3 threatens ♕xb8 and ♕xg7 mate—1...♕xe8 2 ♕xb8 wins the exchange.

Queen Fork with Mate Threat

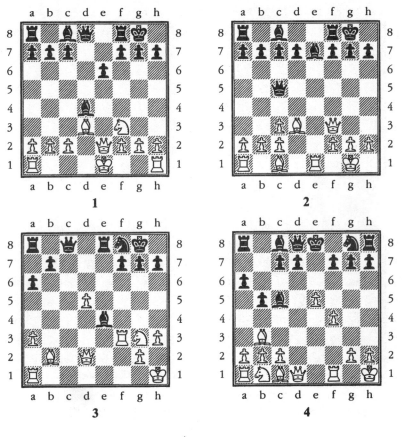

1

2

3

4

Answers

1: 1 ♕e4 threatens ♕xh7 mate and the bishop on d4 for a second time. Notice that 1 ♗xh7+ ♔xh7 2 ♕e4+ followed by ♕ or ♘xd4 wins a pawn.

2: 1 ♕e4 wins the bishop on e7 (attacked twice) because of the threat of ♕xh7 mate. 1 ♗xh7+ ♔xh7 2 ♕e4+ followed by ♕xe7 wins a pawn.

3: 1 ♕d4 wins the bishop on e4 (attacked twice) because of the threat of ♕xg7 mate,

4: 1 ♕d5 threatens ♕xf7 mate, a bishop and a rook!

Knight Forks

Knight forks are of the same types as queen forks but I have split them into only two groups. In the first group are forks with check. In the second group are forks where a piece is attacked and mate threatened or a fork on two or more pieces.

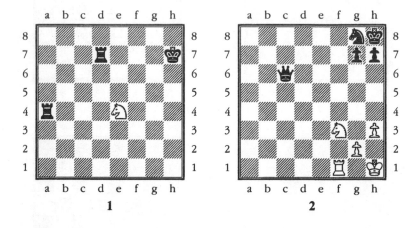

1

2

1: 1 ♘f6+ forces a king move after which White plays ♘xd7. 1 ♘c5 forks the rooks. Black can move one rook to defend the other but he will still lose the exchange. See diagrams on pages 159-161 for forks with check.

2: 1 ♘e5! threatens ♘f7 mate and ♘xc6. Black loses his queen. For knight forks without check see diagrams on pages 162-164.

Knight Forks with Check

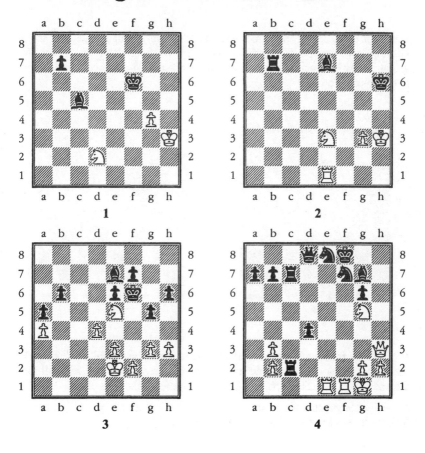

Answers

1: 1 ♘e4+ wins the bishop.

2: 1 ♘f5+ wins the bishop which is now attacked twice.

3: 1 ♘d7+ wins the pawn on b6. 1 ♘g4+ ♔g6 or ♔g7 wins nothing.

4: 1 ♘e6+ wins the queen.

Knight Forks with Check

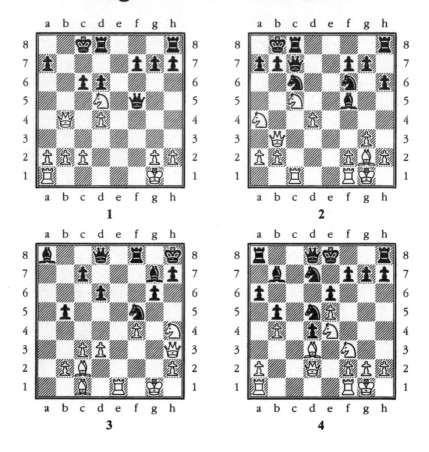

1

2

3

4

Answers

1: 1 ♘e7+ forks king and queen.

2: 1 ♘a6+ ♔a8 (the pawn is pinned!) 2 ♘xc7+.

3: 1 ♘xg6+ wins the exchange (as well as the g-pawn!). The h-pawn is pinned.

4: 1 ♘d6+ followed by ♘xb7.

Knight Forks with Check

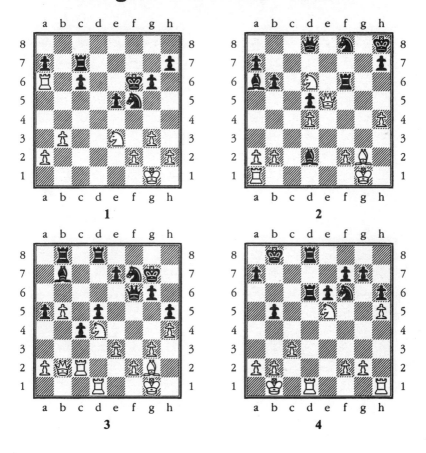

1

2

3

4

Answers

1: The c-pawn is pinned by the rook on a6. 1 ♘d5+ wins the black rook.

2: The black rook is pinned. 1 ♘f7+ wins the black queen.

3: 1 ♘e6+! (the black queen is now pinned!) followed by ♘xd8.

4: 1 ♘c6+! ♖xc6 2 ♖xd8+ wins the exchange. If Black plays anything else then White has ♘xd8. Notice that 1 ♘xf7?? (a fork) loses a rook after 1...♖xd1+.

Knight Forks without Check

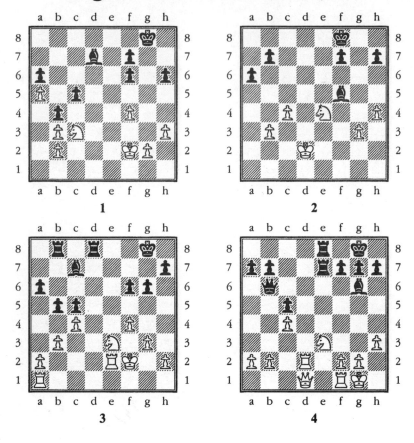

1   **2**

3   **4**

Answers

1:   1 ♘e4 wins one of the two attacked pawns.

2:   1 ♘d6 forks bishop and b-pawn.

3:   1 ♘d5 forks bishop and f-pawn.

4:   1 ♘d5 wins the exchange.

Knight Forks without Check

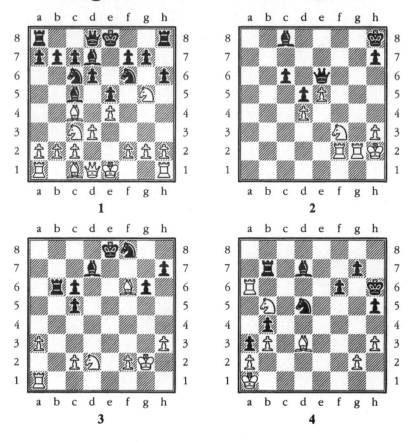

1 **2**

3 **4**

Answers

1:   1 ♘xf7 wins a pawn and the exchange. 1 ♗xf7+ wins only a pawn and after 1...♚e7, White has two pieces attacked.

2:   1 ♘g5!! threatens ♘xe6 and ♘f7+ which will win the queen at least, to prevent mate.

3:   1 ♘c4! attacks and wins the rook because Black must prevent ♘d6 mate!

4:   1 ♘d6! threatens ♘xb7 and ♘f7 mate!

Knight Forks without Check

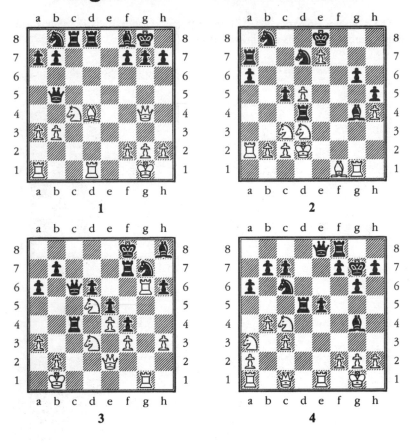

1

2

3

4

Answers

1: 1 ♘d6! forks queen and rook. If 1...♖xd6 then 2 ♕xc8 and if 1...♗xd6?? then 2 ♕xg7 mate!

2: The a-pawn is pinned. 1 ♘b5 forks the rooks.

3: The d-pawn is pinned by the rook on g6. 1 ♘xe5!

4: 1 ♘e3 and Black's best is ♗e6 or ♕d7 giving up the exchange.

Other Forks

The diagrams on pages 166-171 show forks by rooks, bishops, pawns and kings. Sample positions are shown below.

Rook Forks

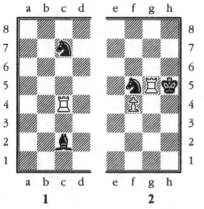

1   **2**

Bishop Forks

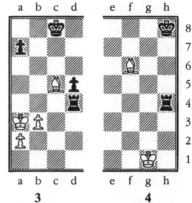

3   **4**

Pawn Forks   ### King Forks

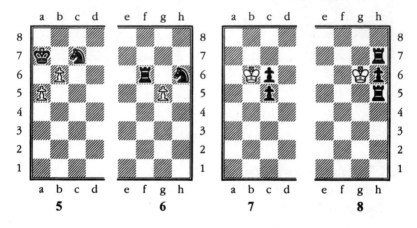

5   **6**   **7**   **8**

Follow the page headings.

Rook Forks

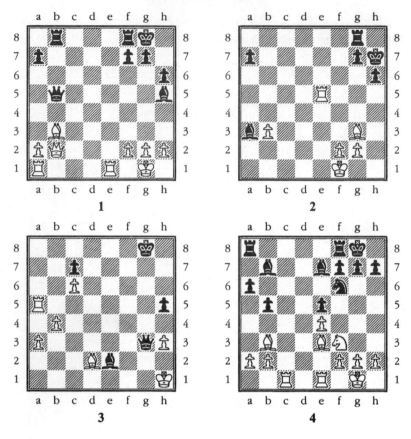

1

2

3

4

Answers

1: 1 ♖e5 wins the black bishop.

2: 1 ♖a5 wins the a-pawn.

3: 1 ♖g5+ wins the queen.

4: 1 ♖c7 wins a bishop.

Rook Forks

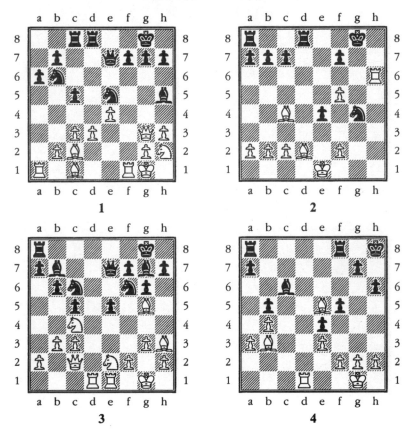

1

2

3

4

Answers

1: 1 ♖f5 wins a piece—the knight is attacked twice.

2: The black f-pawn is pinned. 1 ♖g6+! wins the knight.

3: The knight on f6 is pinned. 1 ♖d7! wins the bishop on b7.

4: The pawn on g7 is pinned so 1 ♖d6! threatens ♖xc6 and ♖xh6 mate!

Bishop Forks

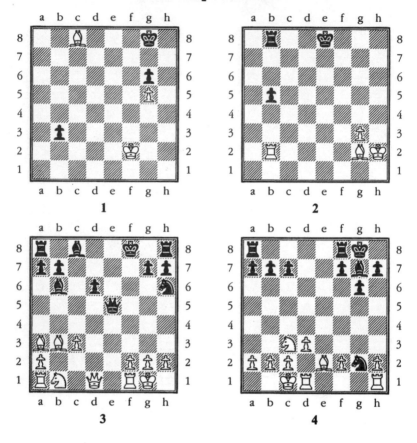

1 **2**

3 **4**

Answers

1: 1 ♗e6+ wins the b-pawn.

2: 1 ♗c6+ wins the b-pawn because it is now attacked twice.

3: 1 ♗xd6+ wins the queen.

4: 1 ♗f3 forks knight and b-pawn.

Bishop Forks

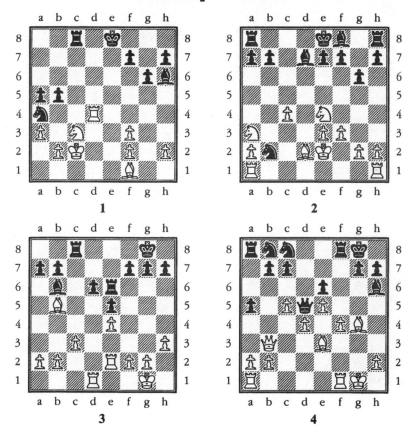

1

2

3

4

Answers

1: 1 ♗xb5+ wins the black knight.

2: 1 ♗c3 forks knight and rook.

3: 1 ♗d7

4: 1 ♗xe6+ wins the black queen.

Pawn Forks

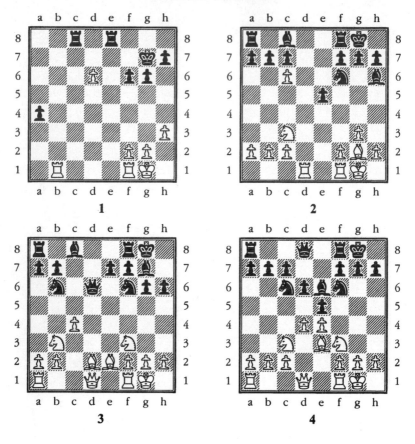

1

2

3

4

Answers

1: 1 d7 wins a rook.

2: 1 cxb7 wins at least a bishop.

3: 1 c5 wins a knight after the black queen moves.

4: 1 d5 wins either a bishop or a knight.

King Forks

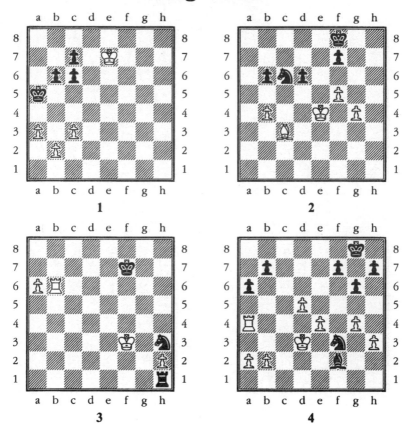

1

2

3

4

Answers

1: 1 ♔d7 wins one of the black c-pawns.

2: 1 ♔d5 wins the d-pawn after the knight moves.

3: 1 ♔g2 followed by ♔xh3 after Black moves his rook.

4: 1 ♔e2 wins a black piece.

Other Ways to Win Pieces

Skewer—a different way to attack two things at once.

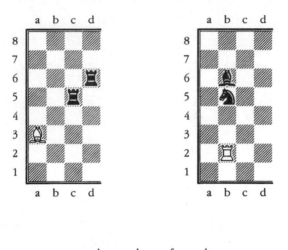

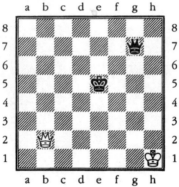

The check on b2 wins the black queen by a skewer.

Remove the Defender

There are two ways to do this—take or force the defender to move to a square where it is not defending.

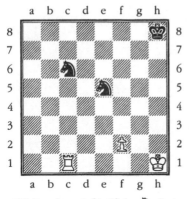

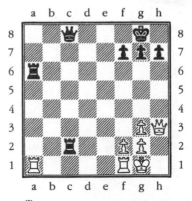

White plays 1 f4. If the ♘e5 stays it is lost to fxe5, but if it moves then ♖xc6. If ♘c4 then ♖xc4.

1 ♕xc8+ removes the defender of the ♖a6. Black must reply ♖xc8 and White plays ♖xa6.

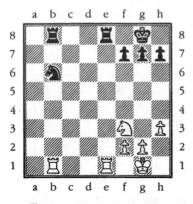

1 ♖xe8+ and Black must reply ♖xe8 allowing ♖xb6.

The black queen is working too hard defending both pieces. White plays ♗xb4 and if Black plays ♕xb4, White can take the bishop for nothing. White could also play ♖xf6 in order to answer ♕xf6 with ♗xb4 but this only wins two pieces for a rook whereas the other move wins a whole piece.

173

Trapping Pieces

Here are some trapped black pieces.

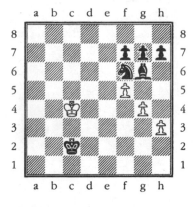

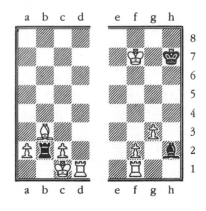

The bishop on g6 is lost, trapped by the white pawns.

(Above left) The black rook was tempted by a pawn. White then played ♗b3 to trap the rook and then castled next move. *(Above right)* The bishop also took a pawn only to be fastened in by g3.

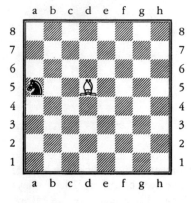

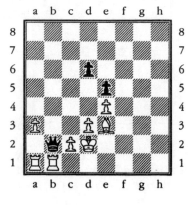

The knight has no safe move, but cannot be taken for the moment.

Even the queen can be trapped after grabbing a pawn.

Scholar's Mate

This is a very common checkmate with beginners and needs looking at carefully. 1 e4 e5 2 ♕h5 ♘c6 3 ♗c4 d6 4 ♕xf7 mate.

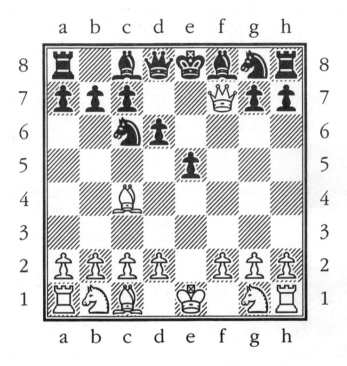

d6 was a very bad move. How many ways could Black have prevented the checkmate?

♕e7, ♕f6, g6, ♘h6. Black could have prevented the checkmate by ♚e7 but after 4 ♕xf7+ ♚d6 his position would be very bad.

It is possible to play this checkmate with slightly different moves: 1 e4 e5 2 ♕h5 ♘c6 3 ♗c4 ♘f6 4 ♕xf7 mate or 1 e4 e5 2 ♗c4 ♘c6 3 ♕f3 d6 4 ♕xf7 mate. There are easy ways to prevent this attack: 1 e4 e5 2 ♕h5 ♘c6 3 ♗c4 g6 or ♕e7; or 1 e4 e5 2 ♗c4 ♘c6 3 ♕f3 ♘f6.